The Forked Tongue
A handbook for treating people badly

Flagg

The Forked Tongue

Copyright © 2000-2008 by Foolish House. All rights reserved worldwide.

Published in association with Power In Practice (www.powerinpractice.com).

TS08SE Special Edition: July 2008

This publication is protected under the US Copyright Act of 1976 and all other applicable international, federal, state and local laws, and all rights are reserved.

Please note that much of this publication is based on personal experience and anecdotal evidence. Although the author and publisher have made every reasonable attempt to achieve complete accuracy of the content in this book, they assume no responsibility for errors or omissions.

USE YOUR HEAD AND YOUR OWN JUDGMENT. Nothing in this book is intended to replace common sense, legal, medical or other professional advice, and is meant to inform and entertain the reader. Use this information as you see fit, and **AT YOUR OWN RISK.**

Any trademarks, service marks, product names or named features are assumed to be the property of their respective owners, and are used only for reference. There is no endorsement or association implied by the use of one of these terms.

If you purchased this book without a cover, you should be aware that this book is stolen property. It was reported as "unsold and destroyed" to the publisher, and neither the author nor the publisher has received any payment for the "stripped book."

A Handbook for Treating People Badly

FOR THE WOLVES WHO RAISED ME

The Forked Tongue

Forward

This is a mixed message.

Mixed messages are a *bad thing*. They confuse, confound, sabotage, and undermine. They *hurt*. To send mixed messages is a damaging, manipulative exploitation of communication. This entire book is constructed of such conflicting ideas; a perverse architecture, built at cross-purposes.

"The Forked Tongue" is what I call a specific argument strategy. It's unfair, unpleasant, frustrating and essentially dishonest. In an upcoming chapter I explain this further, simultaneously warning against it and instructing you exactly how to do it. As I looked over my notes, it occurred to me that this entire effort is akin to warning people about bombs by explaining, step by step, how they are constructed. This is a textbook for treating people badly, and indefensible but for one thing: That is not my intention.

A lot has been written about the duality of what we do. I'll use "BDSM" as it's the most inclusive term I know. Normally, published writing on BDSM addresses the more obvious conflicts for the sake of the outsider. So it's the outsider we address with calming words, (that and the "newbie," a skittish bunny sniffing at the carrot, nose twitching. No sudden moves, lest you scare them) hoping our soothing understatements can pacify the terrible mob waving torches and pitchforks at our gates. *Love* is mentioned a lot, a reassuring word to smooth over the objectionable appearances. *Safety* is part of the litany. Its intoned with a solemnity that suggests more than dedication and reverence but sacrament, as if simply saying it often enough one can make it true.

The Forked Tongue

In focusing on the positive aspects of BDSM, the other accent is the physical, and for good reason. Firstly, it can be explained and instructed. In many cases there are correct ways to do things; these can be illustrated and taught. Methodology, practical applications, advanced instruction, all are available in abundance. Second, it is essentially morally unambiguous to teach people how to do things safely that they are going to do anyway. It's a good thing to help keep them from hurting or killing each other. For the conflicted, it attempts to offset and balance the essential question: *"How can people who care about each other DO those things to each other?"*

The last word in the holy trinity is of Safe, Sane and Consensual *consent*; its many complexities and implications rendered into a simple, cheery black-and-white. And so all the dangerous, murky shadows are dispelled for the sake of the outsider, for the sake of the fearful, and for the sake of those among us who wish it really *was* so simple. For some, the questions are fearsome, the threat of social disapproval terrifying. So when the essential conflict is presented, the basic dichotomy which defines our sexuality, there is a panicked scrambling for answers which make everyone sleep a little easier.

The worst of those answers may be "its only make-believe" because for a wide spectrum of us, it's *not*. In varying degrees, it becomes intensely real. BDSM is treated as a choice, an option, like choosing a flavored lube, colored condom, or kitchen wallpaper. Admittedly, for some people it is. It's worn like cologne, and with as much significance. This is often put forward as the acceptable norm; it's certainly the least troublesome of all the possibilities that BDSM poses. But like most things, it's not that simple. Some of us don't *have* a choice.

We do these things because that's who we are. For some of us, the desires are far more primal and deeply rooted than the physical. For those, I understand and feel a kinship to. Physical acts are simply tools, no matter how elaborate, complex or advanced. The end result is *not* the act. Without the impact of what it makes our partner *feel*, without the deep and murky psychological (and for some, spiritual) depths that we are able to reach, these acts would be hollow mockeries and atrocities. Out of context they are aberrant and criminal; in context they are holy. These things are *who we are*.

And we are without compass. These things are not acknowledged; they are (often rightly) feared. Such desires are shameful, even by the standards of our own community. One of the most startling standards seems to be that just about any physical action can be accepted under the umbrella of "heavy play," even as *art* – provided the mind is never touched. Altered states of consciousness are revered, but intentional alteration abhorred. Blood and bruises no longer mean abuse in the context of these lives, but any touching of the mind or the identity is often greeted with horror. The liberation from our flesh is exhilarating, but the vulnerability of our most essential self is taboo. For some of us that taboo is the only thing that matters. It is the only reason to do this; it is the only thing that feeds us. It defines us.

I do a lot of teaching and public speaking. I bring my instruction to public forums and am heavily invested in TES, a large BDSM support group centered in NYC. Education is a priority there, but often it is slanted very much the same way that instructional books are. I, and others, have had some success in balancing the scales, but it is a continuous effort. There are far too many who are eager to banish the shadows. Part of this crusade means avoiding ambiguities, of disavowing the very duality that makes us vital and whole. At TES, I began to address this duality and these shadows, finding a tremendous response, both locally and nationally. Either because of genuine identification or morbid curiosity, there was a demand for it. The nature of that need became even clearer when I began to discuss the problem with our estranged cousins of the professional dominant community. The pros found the same problem over and over – physical instruction was provided in abundance, while more ambiguous education like psychological instruction was conspicuously absent. I began teaching at NYC houses of Dominance and tailoring some of my lessons to the commercial venue. I also began gathering my notes to publish this book – to fill that niche, that absence, that imbalance.

So here is my offering to my kin: to those who are exploring this same dark territory. It's not just dark to the outsider; it's dark to us, too. Often frightening and confusing, we have to set our own borders to define ourselves as people. Good and whole people worthy of love and acceptance. The condemnation of outsiders is really not the problem; the condemnation to which we subject ourselves is. Despite all this, we are what we are. We need what we need, and we will seek out people to explore with us. When we are lucky, we find them. When we do, we want to act; we want to know what to do to put voice to these urges, hoping to become whole. I can't tell you what to do. I can't answer those questions for anyone else, but I can offer tools for you to find them for yourself. That's what you really want. The easy answers supplied by others will never be satisfying, only you can come to terms with your own hungers.

This is not a 101 or "BDSM for everyone." Actually, this is not really for *anyone*. Most of the things that are in this book I cannot sanction anyone doing to anyone else. Except, of course, that we do, and we will, and we want to. So here are tools to do them well, to do them ethically, and to enact your own, terrible sacraments. We seek to ascend, so we descend.

I called this book a mixed message, a perverse architecture, and so it is. The keystone of this edifice is inscribed within the heart of all these chapters, these words at cross-purpose.

That inscription reads:

*"Here is something you should never do to anyone.
And here is exactly how to do it to someone you care about."*

I truly hope that in the end, it serves it's purpose – to help you and yours be happy. Because truthfully, that is the only thing that makes it's existence excusable. Your joy is my redemption; there is not enough salvation to go around.

Flagg
September 2006

The Forked Tongue

Author's note

I am not enough of a hypocrite to preach about safety. Others are better suited to do that and have done so, far better than I ever could. I do want people to "*play safe*;" I don't want to see anyone unintentionally injured. But there are shades of behavior which cannot be covered by so simple a mantra, or, as I have mentioned, by pretending that people don't do them.

There are slogans. God help us, there are slogans. A lot of people get very caught up in these slogans, apparently confusing the slogan for the fact. We are not going to waste our time there either. In the end, slogans do not matter to this book's intended audience.

There are people out there who modify their bodies; there always have been. This has reached a measure of social acceptance; some of the less intense ventures filtering down to piercing and tattoo parlors all over the United States. It's the stuff of malls and sitcoms now, on that end of the spectrum. But the urge to modify the body reaches far, far further and far deeper than navel rings and nose piercing. Tattoos, implants, amputations, castrations... a bewildering and near infinite variety of expression. The more extreme the mod, the less social acceptance it bears. But make no mistake – people do it anyway, because they *need* to. It is not our place to judge that need, or to decide for them if the need is healthy or proper. We are going to accept that the need simply is. If you can't do that, read no further.

A subset of this community, there are those whose needs require that others do these things to or for them. Again this ranges from simple piercing to tattoos all the way through to major body modifications. This complicates matters, but moves even closer to where the intended audience of this book lives. The creation of a new context for such actions creates a whole crop of questions, and there are so many possible modifications and so many possible contexts that it defies any simple, broad stroke definition. *There is no one answer.*

The same goes for us.

Our contexts are varieties of power exchange. Our currency includes modification of the body, but, more important to this work, the mind. In some cases we are outlaws among outlaws, the context of our needs defying easy molds, definitions and slogans. Our needs do not respect slogans. They are what they are; we are what we are. So for me to preach "safety" in the classical sense is useless. But what we still have between us are two things: Consent and Ethics.

Consent is addressed in most places with the same broad, safe brush and user-friendly colors. It's a simple yes or no, retractable at any time, as ephemeral as wind, rendered meaningless in the endless search for social acceptance and the fear of social consequence. Negotiation is ongoing, endless, and infinitely malleable, with the word "yes" meaning almost nothing, and the word "no" meaning almost everything. Upon utterance of "no," the world is to stop; to hear "yes" is simply permission to wait for the word "no."

Some of us don't see consent this way. Consent is as shifting and shaded a thing as the people who use it, as varied as the relationships that bear it. It is conditional, to be certain, but in public forums we only concern ourselves with the most limiting forms of those conditions – the easy to digest ones, the ones that sound… defensible.

Consent can mean much more than that. Consent can change the parameters of a life. Think about joining the military. Rights as a citizen change or vanish, and the volunteer is subject to an authority which can dictate when and what to eat, how to dress, where to be, what to do, and decide if it is worth it to risk or take your life. You are subject to the will of not just one, but thousands of strangers. Your rights – including your right to leave – are suspended or changed. It's all legal, and it's done every day. It is socially lauded.

Yet somehow, it's different at home.

People become uncomfortable if one chooses to submit oneself to the authority of another, no matter how well known or trusted. They shout about rights and the law as if freedom were not a privilege we enjoy, but a mandatory state we must embrace.

People shout about a lot of things – religion and sexuality come to mind; but there, at least, is room for social dispute in the modern world. Not so consent. Many, many laws and taboos stand to protect us from ourselves, no matter what our natures and needs. To undertake a genuinely power imbalanced relationship appears to take nearly as much planning and subterfuge as a bank heist, with some of the same risks.

Yet we do it anyway. Because we have to, because it's who we are.

Do I advocate a consent dynamic so extreme it transfers the power of life and death into the hands of one partner?

No. What I do believe is that a flag is not the *only* thing that one can pledge their life to, that one can choose to die for.

And therein lie some of the shades of consent. In my relationships, I am most at home with what is termed "blanket consent." The idea is that not every little thing is pre-negotiated, perhaps little or nothing is. My authority extends anywhere I choose to exert it, limited only by the adamant refusal of my servant. That adamant refusal also ends the relationship structure. My friend and peer Sir C terms this act "The right of last refusal." It means you can say no to her, but in so doing, you are ending your part in the structure. To say no to what you don't want is to give up everything you do. These are the terms that feel real to me, that feel genuine and right. This is a form of consent but it demands something that moment-to-moment consent does not:

It demands a very highly developed sense of *ethics*.

Moment-to-moment consent is so common and endorsed so freely because it is *safe*. In a very real way, it is as close to genuine safety as we can aspire to while still doing what we do. The farther you stray from that, the more important ethics become. "Integrity" does not just mean honesty and sincerity. It is also used in terms of "structural integrity". And the more power you genuinely have, the greater your responsibility to maintain that integrity. Your structure has to work.

Most important, you must be absolutely certain that your partner and yourself are entering this structure with the *exact same understanding of what it is*, that the understanding of the consent you share is *identical*. I am working on another project which will get into building and maintaining such structures in more detail (The Core Protocol Seminar), so for the purposes of this book we will narrow your focus to this:

You cannot *trick* your way into the kind of consent necessary to do some of these things; you cannot *wish* your way there. It does not matter how much you want to do them, or what your fantasies are. Your partner must be one of those people who genuinely wants to experience a situation where he or she have no control and very possibly, no way out – and you must be certain they understand exactly what that means and that they are going to be able to handle the experience and its ramifications. If you have *any* doubts about these

things, *stop*. This is risky enough with the right person; with the wrong one it is disastrous.

Remember that the more excited someone is, the more they will consent to. These agreements are worth little or nothing. Be clear. Omit discussions of love, flowers, or forever – those are different conversations, which have nothing to do with the topic at hand. Remember that "I love you, so I'll do anything for you" has a flip side: "If you loved me, how could you treat me this way?"

The tools presented here are in no way limited to the scenarios by which they are explained. The methods laid out in the Interrogation chapter are by no means only useful in interrogations. Once you understand the impact and purpose of any given tool, it's yours, and you'll find your own uses for it; you'll make it your own. These things have repercussions. Make sure that they are what you want, and what you are ready for. It's up to you to be ready, and to put the well-being of the structure and the people in it – yourself included – before the fantasy, before the need. That is your ethical responsibility: When you take the power of choice from someone, then it is only your ethics that keep you both from ruin.

Despite all these truths, people want to do these things. Despite all the risks, people need them, and will do them. So here is a toolbox filled with sharp tools, so that at least you might have the right tool for the right job. These things are presented as tools so that you can mix and match your actions to your needs, so you can act with some idea of what the repercussions might be, and so you are not totally without good tools in an undertaking that is risky enough without guidance. These things are presented because some of you *are going to do them anyway*, and for you this is the best I can offer – and so I do – because no one else will. This is not a *safe* book, but I will do my best to make it an *ethical* one.

The Forked Tongue

Contents

vi   FORWARD

ix   AUTHOR'S NOTE

1   CHAPTER 1: STRUCTURE
     Protocol, Ritual, and Rules

13   CHAPTER 2: HYPNOFETISH
     A Mind is a Terrible Thing to Waste

23   CHAPTER 3: MINDFUCKS
     Now You See It, Now You Don't

45   CHAPTER 4: HUMILIATION
     Nothing Cuts Like Words

59   CHAPTER 5: CONDITIONING
     The Hammer of the Mind

77   CHAPTER 6: INTERROGATION
     As Old as Secrets

91   CHAPTER 7: THE LAST WORD
     Life, Death, and the Edge

95   AFTERWARD
     Unalterable, Unforgettable, Unforgivable

The Forked Tongue

Chapter I: Structure
Protocol, Ritual, and Rules

When building anything to last, you start with the foundation; and that foundation must be sound.

When one looks at the written agreements and contracts that the BDSM universe vomits forth with appalling frequency (and equal predictability), there are certain ideas that crop up repeatedly: love, protocol, rituals, and lists of rules. As the easiest place to mine these gems is the internet, one can almost exclusively find them on ghastly web pages with black or even worse "dungeon brick" backgrounds, horrible colored fonts, burning torch gifs, and rose motifs entwined through every margin. This should tell us something. Unfortunately, when seeking some idea of guidance in D/s structure, that's pretty much the extent of the available reference. Even the best of them are simply accountings of what the author wants, how the author does things; to my knowledge there are no suggestions on how to successfully forge a structure for yourself.

Not a lot of thought has gone into making structure workable, and without a common language, such ideas are even less likely to be communicated with any success. So I'm going to break down the vocabulary of the D/s "contract," and offer a set of tools to create a workable structure. This does not lend itself to creating the hot and sexy document of ownership that gets everybody all tingly; in and of itself it's likely to be as exciting as real estate law, if considerably shorter and less complex.

The Forked Tongue

When I first started venturing into ownership, one of my peers introduced her written set of guidelines for those who would serve her. It was an imposing and concise document, as she is an imposing and concise woman. I was impressed by what she'd done, and set about trying to commit my own ideas to paper. It was a difficult process, and in the end I had a document about eight pages long. I had broken things down to three "protocols" with three subsets for each – formal, public, and informal. I had headings for voice, body, demeanor, "rituals," you name it. Pages of serious looking pronouncements, giving the appearance of a stern and demanding Master with deliberate rules and expectations, for every circumstance. I was suitably proud of my work and set about training those under me to meet these shining standards. I had a contract. I was *legit*. I had *arrived*.

Nonsense.

The first error I had made was to think that *more* was *better*. Competing with all I'd read and with the excellent documentation of the aforementioned woman, Sir C, I wrote myself into a corner. It took me awhile to realize that I had overcomplicated my most elemental urges because I wanted *pages*: a document that made me feel secure, as if it were proof that I knew what I was doing. Some part of me was afraid that someone was going to demand proof that I was a Dominant like a passport at the border – but I would be ready, because I had stuff *on paper*. Insecurity is no motivation to do anything, much less structure an essential part of your life around. Now, there was nothing wrong with all these guidelines *per se*, but they were created for the wrong reasons, and I eventually found that they only got in the way. In a sense I provided these rules, the rules governed the servants… and I was out of the loop. There was no organic connection possible with this document between us. In a sense I was hiding behind it, for as long as I had these papers, I rarely had to actually take the risk of actively *dominating* anyone. The papers did it for me, except, of course, they did nothing of the sort. In the end it was a learning experience, one of many. Once I wised up, I boiled my eight pages down to five lines which have served me ever since.

I mention these pitfalls not because I assume anyone else will have the same issues, but as an illustration of the many singular, individual ways we can go wrong in such matters – it's not always the writing that's the problem, but *why* it was written. However, there is no way to anticipate all the possible motivations which can trip us up, so I posit my own personal experience by way of object lesson and leave it at that.

As odd as it may seem, what works for me does not necessarily work for everybody, which prevents me from the simple solution of simply telling everybody what to do. Pity, that. So I've rendered what I've learned into some clear definitions and guidelines for creation of a structure that works – concise, to the point, and with a language that is both internally and externally consistent. That way, in future chapters when I refer to your structure, protocols, rules, or rituals we are all speaking the same language.

LESS IS MORE

As you begin thinking about what you want, you might find that either you have a list which is pages long, filled with all kinds of cool stuff, or only a few lines and you are drawing a blank. Do not be dismayed if you can't think of an imposing shopping list. That's just fine. If you have a long list in front of you, you have a lot more work to do.

As we go through these headings, you are going to be confronted with urgings to eliminate all kinds of things that upon first glance, might seem vital to you and your vision of how your servants should behave. I am not telling you to abandon the things you want; I am suggesting that a service contract defining the structure that binds your servant to you and your service may not be the place for them. You will have all the time and space you want to create as elaborate a bible of expectations and responsibilities as you want – but all those things should fit *within* the framework you are laying out here, not be *part* of it.

It is the difference between building the house and hanging the curtains. This is the document that sets out parameters: situations that may dictate an exception or alteration to your authority, commitments you make to uphold your side of the structure, what defines those responsibilities, definitions of your servant's role in your household, the acceptance of deliberate physical or mental changes or markings, what areas of the servant's life your authority does and does not extend to, and the like. Hard data, and enforceable.

Anything more than this is extraneous, and a complication to the effort. There will be a time and place to outline ritual expectations such as forms of address, signs of respect and deference such as kneeling, and the details of service. All the fun stuff comes later. You have to *build* the house before you can decorate it.

So what are you left with? A nuts and bolts, unadorned and utterly glamourless document dealing with mundane but vital issues, outlining the terms of service, which are going to impact both your lives. The extent of authority must be clear. No gray areas. It can encompass all or part of the servant's life. It may or may not address the servant's health, safety and financial stability, or it may provide situations where other things such as family supercede or alter the existence of the structure – I don't care. What I care about is that whatever is addressed is enforceable, clear, and well defined. The more you write, the more work you have to do to meet these qualifications, so whenever possible, keep it clear and simple. This is the heart of your structure, and the final arbiter of the extent of your authority. Treat it as such. This is the place for you to enact Soulhuntre's Law: "Minimum amount of words, maximum amount of information."

The first step is getting rid of abstracts. If you cannot enforce it, if it cannot be materially produced, and worst of all, if it cannot be realistically provided – lose it. For example, you cannot legislate how someone feels, only how he or she acts, and to some extent, how they appear. Some Dominants are willing and capable of putting in the work of altering how someone thinks, but that cannot be legislated on a piece of paper. By way of example, I'll refer to my friend Sir C's "Demeanor Clause." It does not demand that the people serving her "be happy," it commits them to maintaining a pleasant demeanor at all times when in her company. Thus, she does not attempt to control the abstract (their feelings), only the concrete (the expression of those feelings).

WHAT'S LOVE GOT TO DO WITH IT?

Love is great, but it does not help in building a D/s foundation. In fact, from top's side, it tends to be a complication. It may be *why* you are together, but we are not dealing with that right now; we are dealing with *how* you are together. For the purposes of this discussion, it is counter-intuitive and distracting. If love is present, it does not need inclusion; love is an abstract and we are working with concrete concepts. If not, a document can't make it appear, so why mention it? Don't confuse what you are doing with why you are doing it. If love must be mentioned in your document, make it in a separate area, and my suggestion is: Do not phrase anything so that behavior hinges on feeling. To say that this agreement is "because of our love" or some such suggests that if someone is feeling unloved, his or her responsibilities are somehow secondary to that feeling. This is not what you want. It makes your structure reliant on mood and perception, and is akin to building on a swamp – no steady foundation.

So, strike all mention of the abstract and the unenforceable. If you cannot see yourself realistically issuing something as an absolute and affirmative

The Forked Tongue

command, ("Be happy now!" "Sexual excitement now!" "Love this! Schnell!") it might not be appropriate. Sexual availability is enforceable, sexual excitement – not so much. Emotions, involuntary responses (I've seen a document that demands erect nipples.) and, especially treacherous, love – should be struck from your list.

PROTOCOL

What it is, and what it is not.

This word is vastly misused, and seems to mean, "Whatever I tell you" to a lot of people. We are going to address protocol in the more military/ diplomatic/ scientific sense: a statement addressing *what to do*. This may not sound so different at first, but I mean it quite literally – only positive statements concerning behavior and reaction to situation. No negatives. Think of it in terms of bomb disposal protocol. When it says, "cut the red wire" it means *exactly* that, and addresses the question of everything else by default. No, you don't cut the green wire yet, it says cut the red one, *so that's what you do.* So in drafting protocols, keep your statements as orders of what to do, which will tell your servant what not to do by default. Protocol means: "in this situation/for this result, do *this.*"

Resist the impulse to start piling gestures and clutter in here. These things are important, the guiding program for what you wish your servant to achieve without your immediate guidance even in your absence. This is about priorities and decision-making, a program for how to live and how best to serve. It takes some thought, as these protocols are going to steer the direction of your servant's existence in relation to you. Though not quite graven in stone, these are the "Ten Commandments" of their service; save the frivolity for later.

Rules

If protocol is "always," rules are "never." Another list that is likely to be short if addressed correctly, we're going to treat rules as the place for taboos, those few things you don't want your servant to ever do. Try not to make them situational, and try not to make them redundant with the protocols. If you have listed "full and honest disclosure at all times" as a protocol, there is no need to write "never lie to me" as a rule. However, blanket policies of "never lie" might make an appropriate rule if your authority structure extends into your servant's dealings with others, and thus a valid rule. In general, a well-written set of protocols will preclude a need for an elaborate set of rules.

Rituals

Finally, the fun stuff. But again, less tends to be more here. Be careful what you wish for, as rituals can be a real monkey's paw. The issue is this: Anything you assign, you must diligently and continuously enforce; the more elaborate and arcane, the more persistent and troublesome you make these, the more you'll pay for it in the end. If you let it go, let it slide… that means that it does not matter, that what your servant does – and therefore your *servant* – does not matter, that your commands and edicts do not matter, that *you* do not matter. **It is an instant devaluation of the currency of power.**

So, in order to keep your rituals living, useful, and vital, you need to determine: Out of all of your notions of what is right for you, is this important? Is this symbol, this gesture an essential part of your identity, a keystone of what you want to build with this particular servant? Would your interactions with this servant seem incomplete without it? Would you be willing to enforce its enaction, to the point of dismissal if it is ignored?

Are you willing to put in the effort to *fight* for it?

The Forked Tongue

By way of example, those under me refer to me as "Sir." If they don't, or won't – they are gone. It's a small thing in the scheme of things, but to me it is that important. I am willing to put in the effort to discipline the lazy, timid, or forgetful or dismiss the obstinate. I am willing to *fight* for it. To me, it is essential. A servant will not sleep in the same bed with me; if they are emotionally intimate with me they sleep on the floor by my bed, if not, they sleep elsewhere. Anything else would feel very wrong to me, so I maintain it.

So with this in mind, I advise you to choose only those rituals that are truly important to you. The more rituals you have, the more time and energy you are committing to observing and enforcing them. You can bury yourself, paint yourself into a corner, and in effect, become as obliged to them as your servants are; a slave to your own rituals. Odds are good that is not what you really want.

Before we move on to a practical way of combining all these elements, just a note: *If a ritual is not working for you, get rid of it or change it.*

I have known some people who worry that changing their rituals might make them look indecisive. Well, if you dither around frivolously, unable to leave well enough alone, you probably will. But the alternative is worse. A ritual that does not please you is empty at best, and destructive at worst. If the servant under you is striving to please, yet by doing exactly as you have instructed fails to do so, that mixed message is destructive to the faith that binds servant to superior. If it does not work for you, get rid of it.

Putting it all together

Some people like to write things down to organize them, make them concrete. It can also be a handy reference and teaching tool. I'll offer a short form system to help keep your ideas in order:

First, decide if you are going to have one mode of your protocol, or more. (Now, we are dealing with rituals here, but rituals fit *within* protocol – "If this is the situation, *do this*.") These are commonly referred to as *high* and *low* protocol; some people add a middle protocol, making *first, second* and *third*. You can go even farther, assigning terms like formal/informal if you feel the need to get really complicated. Your call, but I still suggest that **Less is More**. We are going to keep our examples fairly simple, and work with three modes: High, Middle and Low; but you are going to make as many or as few modes as suit your needs.

Now you decide on your areas of behavior – let's say *action, attention, speech*, and *priority*.

Now we have a table to make your notes easier:

Protocol	Action	Speech	Attention/Priority
1st (High)	Kneel if I stand still; stand to my right if I sit	Begin and end all sentences with "Sir"	Designated guests first, then attend me
2nd (Middle)	Stand / walk behind me and to my right	Address me as "Sir"	My needs first
3rd (Low)	Location is irrelevant	Address me as "Sir" unless in vanilla company	As situation demands

So, what we have are rituals and designations of priority that are dependent on context and situation. If these things don't change, (Such as "Always sleep on the floor by my bed" or "Always keep my refrigerator stocked with iced tea and ice") then there is no need for a table. Rules also rarely need to be fit into such a device. "Never let my glass stay empty" stands alone.

On the whole, with the exception of the shifting, context-sensitive ideas, most of this does not *need* to be written out. Is it really necessary for you to put your iced tea into your contract? It's an order, just issue it. If you start dithering with details such as iced tea, then you are on the road to putting in every other little thing you can think of. If food service and attendance are important – shopping, cooking, serving – then perhaps there is room for that as a written issue; because anything you put in writing is going to be given a special significance by your servant, and is likely to be prioritized higher than other orders. If you are a contract type of person, be aware that orders will be obeyed, but written specifics define a servant's existence in your household, and thus are likely to always be given priority unless you specify otherwise.

In closing, I strongly suggest that you don't get carried away. Paper is meaningless; it's the dynamic interaction between your servants and yourself that matters. Writing things out is just making a map for yourself of where you want to go; don't confuse the map for the journey.

Why bring any of this up at all?

Firstly, in order to create a common language between us. However, there is something far more important than that.

I am going to be referring to "structure" a great deal in the upcoming chapters, using it as the universal yardstick by which ideas and actions are undertaken or allowed. Just because I have outlined the potentials of a written rule set does not mean I advocate it. Not everyone wants or needs one. A good friend of mine goes with "I tell you what I want, you do it." It works, and it suits him and the people who choose to be under him.

I wrote a complex protocol, used it for years, and disposed of it, finding that I really only needed five guidelines – anything else, I direct as I choose. Yet another friend has more than a dozen pages of exacting micromanagement, and it suits her perfectly and functions flawlessly.

However, what is in common here is that there is a *structure* in every case, boundaries and guidelines of one sort or another, in some cases defined only by their absence. It is *imperative* that you are clear on what your structure allows, as many of the ideas I present in upcoming chapters may be things that cross lines that you may not have really considered when first accepting service from those under your authority.

Most critical of all, however, is this: most of these tools and scenarios I am addressing not only preclude moment-to-moment consent, they cannot coexist with it *at all*. In some cases traditional communication is impossible, in others incompatible with the end goals. Without the check-ins of traditional consent, without safewords or time-outs, you are left only with your structure, with the **integrity** of that structure, to keep you from ruin.

And even that is no guarantee.

The Forked Tongue

Chapter 2: Hypnofetish
A Mind is a Terrible Thing to Waste

Since *The Cabinet of Dr. Caligari*, millions of people have been aware of the sinister and erotic potential of hypnosis. Like a magic power, unfathomable forces dangle and dance a helpless victim on invisible strings, subjugated to the merest whispers of the mesmerist's voice... or so popular fictions would portray it. The truth is that image is simultaneously correct and misguided; many of the clichés are true, but only under certain conditions. Amusingly enough, the application of hypnosis may have been perverted all the way back to its popular discovery by Franz Mesmer. His female subjects, most often being treated for "hysteria" and "the vapors," reported that his technique involved soothing, stroking, and caresses culminating in a pleasurable "explosion." It seemed to work, as his subjects were much more relaxed after their treatment at the hands of the good Dr. Mesmer. Smiling and eager for a return treatment, in fact.

I have mentioned that traditionally, focus is on the physical, thus we are going to start with the purely mental. No whips, no chains, no limits to where you can take your subject. Infinitely versatile, hypnosis – within its limitations – can invoke nearly any response or state in your subject. However, understanding those limitations is vital.

Just a note – I have seen hypnotism horribly misused, causing harm and distress. Like any topic presented here, I am not going to moralize; those who are ethical will remain so, those who are not will be unmoved. So instead I'll address the guidelines we have set for ourselves previously: be

The Forked Tongue

certain that your end result falls within the boundaries of your structure, and judge conservatively.

What is hypnotism?

To define hypnosis, it's far better to start with what it is not. Hypnosis is what a subject does to themselves – not what you do to them. It is said that all hypnosis is self-hypnosis; it's simply easier with a guide. As that guide, it is within your power to create mental systems and structures that effectively reinforce your position. While it is true that subjects will "only do what they want to do," that is actually a very flexible set of standards. What people consciously think they want, and what they desire in other states of consciousness, are often very different things. In addition, by associating concepts, one might be able to bypass certain types of resistance. So, the effects you can have on a subject are far more extensive than the simplistic "only what they want to do" idea. On the other hand, deeply felt convictions and beliefs, fears, and desires may prove inviolate to change – but that does not make them useless.

I am not going to attempt an in-depth dissertation of the hows and whys of hypnosis. Like so many other things, such information is readily available from those infinitely more qualified. I am going to focus on a basic walkthrough, some layman's explanations, and the sorts of results one can reasonably expect with an average subject.

Everyone slips into hypnotic states all the time; they are a normal part of human functioning. Think of time spent walking or driving a long, familiar route. Often you are home before you know it. The mind wanders, but you can't really account for all that time... there are blind spots – expanses of time and distance you don't remember. These are, essentially, hypnotic states. Hypnotism is intentionally bringing these trances about, in oneself or another. These guided trances can lead to even deeper states, suggestible states where one can step in and create powerful systems. I find this to be an exceedingly intoxicating process, as challenging as it is intimate and versatile. To me, it feels like power.

I wish I could tell you surefire methods of determining who is a good subject and who is not, but I really can't. Some people – a small minority – just don't go under when coached in the traditional way; they are simply poor subjects. If you notice that someone is easily suggestible in waking life, odds are good they will be a good hypnosis subject, but there are no guarantees.

The first step is *"induction,"* the process of intentionally easing into an altered, suggestible state of consciousness. Ideally, you want a quiet and comfortable place, although the experienced hypnotist may be able to invoke these states under wildly different conditions. Stage magicians doing hypnosis shows, for example, use the high stress conditions of a subject standing before lights and a huge audience of strangers to cause the subject to effectively *flee* into the safety of a hypnotic state. We are going to focus on a simpler, more classical method – the countdown.

Once your outward location is suitable, you then have to consider an *inner* setting. Imagery is exceedingly effective in helping induce the hypnotic desired state; it is engaging, interesting, almost universal, and an effective distraction from the goal. If the subject is concerned with reaching this place to please their superior, they can often generate a self-defeating tension that sabotages their own effort. The misdirection of imagery tends to keep the subject engaged, and therefore facilitates the process. However, what images you invoke in your descriptions can be critical. These images should be familiar and comfortable, suiting your subject's preferences and dispositions. Talking about sinking in a warm pool of clear, calm water is not going to relax a subject with a fear of drowning. Elevators, stairs … many of the common induction images are not universally ideal. Know your subject, and use appropriate descriptions. I know a subject for whom most all descriptions of descent – the traditional type of coaching – are negative. For her, I abandon the "descent" image and describe lying sunbathing on the beach, growing warmer and drowsier, counting the sound of waves. Don't get locked into one type of image – the goal is *relaxation*.

Once you have chosen suitable outer and inner surroundings, what do you do with them?

The actual induction process is simple; occupying and relaxing the mind of the subject until he or she drops off into a fugue state, a suggestible trance wherein you can set about your suggestions and instructions. The classic image is the watch or shiny object, but that is not actually necessary. What all the methods have in common are focus and rhythm. Focus can be supplied by a device, such as the classic swinging watch, or by the guided imagery we have discussed, engaging the imagination and diverting the focus of the subject inward, away from the distractions of the outside world. The watch also supplies rhythm, a steady metronome that numbs the senses. This can be supplied easily with steady counting, evenly interspersed with guided imagery and relaxing, soothing speech. Examples of such scripts can be found at www.hypnosis.org, as well as many other sources.

Once your subject is under, many of the same rules apply. If you are using guided imagery, I suggest maintaining consistency both in the induction and the imagery used. For some, abrupt changes are jarring, possibly confusing. Keeping the type of person your subject is in mind, create a way to symbolize the relay of information – books for the bibliophile, a large darkened movie theatre, a computer screen – some device to maintain the visual imagination and engage positive connotations. In the case of the medical fetishist, I invoked an operating room, and the suggestions I implanted took the form of surgical implants – unorthodox to be certain, but images that this particular subject responded very favorably to. Transition from induction to suggestion should be handled simply but consistently, in accordance with these ideas – guidance from the beach to a beach house with a book on the table, for example. Don't complicate the transition; just a simple shift of images is all that is needed. The more elaborate you make this transition, the more complicated and distracting it becomes for you and your subject. In addition, if you are going to be making this into a ritual, it is important that you remain consistent from induction to induction – if you skip or forget your details due to over complication, it will bother your subject, disturbing their descent into a suggestible, pliable state.

The essential tool in this entire process is the rhythmic focus of a countdown or count-out. It's steady, progressive, and easy to pair with imagery through the idea of the destination. Down the stairs or floor-by-floor of the descending elevator, you can inform them that at the arrival of the destination number, they will be completely relaxed, deeply asleep. An odd note is that counting backwards seems to allow people to ease into this state, counting forwards seems to create a slight anxiety, due to the potential open-endedness of the count. People have said that counting upward seems to feel like a burden, while counting backwards feels like the lessening of that burden. Set a middling number to count from – twenty is usually good, not too short to allow you use of as much soothing imagery as you feel comfortable with, not so long that you grow bored or worse, lose count.

Count slowly, steadily, interspersing your count with consistent images and approaching goals, until finally, you are there and your assurances that they will reach a given state become statements that they *have* reached it. If their slow, steady breathing and drowsy agreement support this, you've arrived.

Now what?

Before we set about creating a suggestion, you should figure out for yourself what effects you want. Start with simple ideas, and allow yourself to add to the work as both you and your subject gain in confidence. There is no way for me to list all the possible diversions hypnofetish can offer – it is as varied as every one's individual, intensely personal kink. So, I will instead discuss some of the ends I have seen it put to and allow you to contemplate the possibilities for yourselves.

Some people enjoy the fugue state itself, leaving the subject in a "zombie like" state. This state can endure for a surprisingly long time, depending on your subject. I first stumbled upon hypnofetish (quite accidentally, when my first servant became exceedingly suggestible after prolonged multiple orgasms, and I quickly learned to exploit it.) She spent the night and the next day at work in a light trance state, functioning and responding appropriately to stimulus – but with no memory of the time spent after she was awakened to normal consciousness. In effect your subject becomes more obedient and focused, usually possessed of near infinite patience, and no recall of the events that you do not allow. (Note that different people trance to different depths, stay under for varying lengths, and react individually to stimuli; again none of this is absolute for everyone.) One Dominant of my acquaintance enjoys putting a servant under, having an extensive physical scene – flogging, for example – and then waking them without immediate memory; he then has them recall and re-experience the sensations he inflicted upon command at a later time.

I, personally, am *far* more inspired by the power of post-hypnotic suggestion.

The single most common usage I have seen is the "orgasm on command." As cliché as it is entertaining, (especially in a crowded movie theatre or shopping mall), it seems to have a near universal appeal to the dominants

I know who use the tool, myself included. Applicable as either punishment or a reward, it tends to carry an elemental message of control, an indication of the potentially mythic powers that the dominant must have to bypass biology, time and inconvenience, summoning a visceral experience from nowhere with but a word or a gesture. Other things I have seen are commands which snap a subject to attention, inflict phantom pain or other sensations, or cause immobility.

So much more is possible to create. A change in surroundings causing the subject to perceive him or herself to be in any time, setting or location that moves you. Reminders of their station in everyday things, such as picking up a pen, seeing a color or hearing a song. Reinforcements of priorities, protocols, rules and rituals. Memories of events that never happened. I have yet to discover an end to the possibilities. One of my favorite things is to "install" a fetish – boots, oral sex, whatever it is that moves me – and control the intensity on a scale from one to ten, ten making the desire blinding and eclipsing all else. Good fun.

What works well varies from subject to subject. Unlike magic spells and super powers, hypnotic suggestions require maintenance and can fade over time or disuse. The more often they are reinforced, the stronger and more inescapable they feel, but unlike true conditioning, they can fade quickly or dissolve abruptly, especially during time of great stress. Hypnosis is personal, not chemical; as such suggestions can be "drowned out" by stress or strong emotion, in effect like a radio signal being drowned out by static and interference – the "Signal-to-Noise" ratio. Diligent reinforcement can help offset this, but nothing is proof against it.

A third popular type of hypnoplay is the "alternate persona," a personality or identity who behaves differently, sees themselves differently, thinks, reacts, and may even think of themselves differently than your subject is in waking life. The "bimbo," a brainless, giggling sex machine, often deliberately, comically stupid is a popular fetish, with dozens of websites and discussion groups on the subject. The sex robot, the slave raised from birth who knows no other life – all of these things allow a totally immersive fantasy, liberating the servant from day-to-day inhibitions in many cases. It can even allow the superior to experience things that they are self conscious about or feel might erode their authority; I know of a hypnotop who created a dominant sadist persona in his partner, who had no memory of those times. That way he could bottom to her, yet she would be unconflicted bottoming to him in her waking state.

Different people fetishize different elements of hypnosis. Some people are into the counting out process more than the results. Many servants enjoy the count-down method for the attention and the loss of control; for some the countdown experience is an end in itself and a fetishized experience. I know of some who find the blackout – the mystery and retroactive feeling of utter loss of control – equally intoxicating. Some are moved by the power the superior seems to wield, no matter what the manifestation. It is as individual as your subject.

Much like the structure you are working within, you can create a sort of structure within the mind of your subject. For example, one of my favorite things is to create a "backdoor," a single command that bypasses the countdown and induction, snapping the subject into an immediate trance where suggestions can be made, anytime, anyplace. It also allows me to use the countdown as a reward or intimacy, rather than a time consuming necessity. Positive ideas or concepts can be used to reinforce suggestion; core ideas which move the subject are powerful as "anchors." For example, being loved, being owned, a core fetish desire such as feeling small or helpless – most suggestions can be free associated to these feelings, reinforcing the experience of performing the suggested action or experience with a direct correlation to that feeling. Boot worship may not have any conscious association with feeling loved, but you can create that association in the subconscious of your subject to reinforce the suggested desire and action.

Hypnosis is not conditioning in and of itself, although some things can imprint or condition over time, and in deliberate efforts, hypnosis can be helpful. Time, complication, and signal-to-noise can diminish the potency of your efforts, as can illness or overly complicated or contradictory suggestions. Hypnosis is a natural, organic function, essentially a living thing; it is not a machine that keeps running indefinitely. It takes care, maintenance, and empathy – because the better your understanding of your subject, the better your results.

The Forked Tongue

Chapter 3: Mindfucks
Now You See It, Now You Don't

THE BODY IS A FINE PLACE TO START.

Many people, however, think it ends there – and for some, it does. For the rest of us, however, there is something far more. For the deeper player, pain is a tool – and only one of many. The ultimate goal is to profoundly affect the mind – to drastically alter the state of consciousness. Ancient cultures have always known ways to do this – pain, body modification, chemical experience, spiritual rapture – modern primitives keep these traditions alive. There is another art, just as ancient, with roots just as primal, just as visceral: Storytelling. Stagecraft. Shadow plays – the oldest forms of magic.

I am not talking about role-playing. Role-playing is just the opposite of the mindfuck: an agreed-upon enactment, a consensual fantasy, an alternate reality. Mindfucking is not creating an artificial reality; it is deliberately altering the perception of the world we all share without your subject's knowledge, "gaslighting." If you change a person's perception, you change that person's *world*.

The thrill of fear and the unknown are the most primal, elemental experiences we can share. The roller coaster of BDSM, mindplay is the cornerstone of some of the most memorable scenes imaginable. It is my intention to share simple, applicable principles and tools with which you can make someone's world a very, very special place.

This is the place where I am supposed to warn you about all the terrible, terrible things that can happen. So, terrible, terrible things can happen.

There. If you are smart, you knew that, and if you are not, you won't listen. So, my official warning: *don't be stupid.*

If I am to suggest one specific idea to guide you: Let's say you invoke the state you want... what then? What are the consequences of that state? Be careful what you ask for – you might get it.

That being said, let's get back to the point: Why stop with the body? Why pay a middleman, if what you really wish to affect is the *mind*?

Remember, a mind is a terrible thing to waste... when we can hurt that, too.

Definitions:

Illusion: *Creating fodder for misconception*

The goal of *illusion* is not to lie. Ideally, in mindfucking we never lie –not exactly. However, we do strive for our subject to leap to erroneous conclusions, and the art of creating a "leading environment" is *illusion* – the stagecraft of mindfucking.

Suggestion: *Leading to conclusions and false intuitive "leaps"*

Suggestion is the verbal equivalent of the stagecraft of *illusion*: leading statements, misdirection, and disinformation. It is the craft of leading someone to believe something without ever actually saying it. I differ this from lying, as outright falsehoods are to be avoided.

Dread: *Trepidation and anxiety of the unknown, suspected and inferred*

Dread is creeping tension – a crawling sensation of being afraid of *something* – but not knowing what that something *is*. It is the closed box, the darkened closet, the hand behind the back, the knowing smile. Unlike *fear*, dread can be sustained near indefinitely with a little work.

Fear: *Trepidation and anxiety of the known, the immediate and/or the Potential*

While fear might be considered an end in itself – and a worthy one – it is here defined as different from *dread*; fear requires a "known" subject to be afraid of. Fear is *immediate*. The rat in the box, the gloved hand emerging from the closet, the glitter of a scalpel being brought into the light. Unlike *dread*, terror and fear tend to exhaust themselves – and the subject – fairly quickly, and can be difficult to sustain, often changing into anger, passing out, and other escapes.

Trick: *A mindfuck sequence "outside" the rules of the structure*

An arranged event like a surprise abduction (for example) may appear for the duration of the experience to be "outside" the rules of the structure, or unrelated to the structure entirely. Here again, I would advise caution, for although some people *live* for just such an experience, others might consider them damaging or unforgivable.

Things To Know: Know Your *Subject*

The more you know about them, the more effective you can be in leading them.

It seems obvious, but it's worth mentioning a few more times: you need to know your subject. If you want to give somebody a deep, hard, throbbing mindfuck – you have to know what works on them, have some idea of how they will react, and what things you might want to avoid. Like humiliation, Mindplay is different things to different people. What works on one might leave another yawning, and a third never speaking to you again.

It's more than that, however.

It's not just about psychological hot-buttons... it's also about the mundane details you might not ordinarily think about. "The devil is in the details." Is he curious? Would an unopened package in the mail drive him crazy? What if you took it away, and never mentioned it again? What if you refused to discuss it? Acknowledge it? Is she afraid that you are going to bring a certain other Dominant in? What if you keep glancing at her while you are on the phone with him? Smiling – and trying to stifle the smile?

I've said it before: "A submissive's tongue is good for three things; the third one is *shovel*." Given enough time (and rope) a submissive will tell you everything you want to know.

 I swear, they can't *help* it.

So – just *listen*; all the information is there, all you have to do is pay attention.

Be Aware

Discover all the positive and negative motivators you can. Dig for them. Once you know them, apply them judiciously; nothing numbs the senses better than overkill.

Positive motivators: A submissive will jump through hoops in most cases to get their fetishes fulfilled. For many, that very act makes it all that much more exiting. Fetishes are not your only positive motivator; approval, attention, and affection are all powerful when applied to the right people in the right way. Use them sparingly, as they become all the more desirable in their scarcity.

Negative motivators: If you know what works, make sure its presence can be felt. A threat, direct or implied, may be enough. Fear of pain is often more useful than pain itself. Disapproval can be crushing for some, shrugged off by another. The other thing to be aware of is even more powerful negative images... phobias, for example. If your boy is terrified of cockroaches, that is absolutely fair game in many cases for an ideal mindfuck. Bringing actual cockroaches into a scene might be clearly outside of a structure's limits, but the *dread* that there *might* be a cockroach in the room where he is lying blindfolded... that's quite another thing.

Know your *Goals*

Be clear in your aims from the outset. This is stagecraft – you have to be three steps ahead.

The goal is similar to writing, painting, or any other act of creation: you have to know what you want to create from the outset, and then work towards that end. Try not to get bogged down in the fetishistic details at first – it's not about the toys or the tools, it's about the state of mind you are setting out to invoke.

Work backwards: What do you *want*? Panic? Terror? Creeping dread? Paranoia? What state of mind do you want your subject to be in, in the end? And, once that is achieved, what are you going to do with them? A good mindfuck is not over until the curtain is drawn back and you get to take your bow, after all. (More on this later.)

If you know your subject, you'll have some idea of what tools might work, and what mental state you are seeking. Work backwards, asking yourself: "What would cause such a reaction? How long do I want this to go on? How much time do I have? Do I have assistance? What assets do I have to make this happen?" Write a list, if you can – it will be handy as you get ideas later on. Once you get a taste for this, you'll be doing it again.

Be especially careful the nature of the event you are considering, and its potential effects, the reactions it may cause. A mindfuck can make a submissive feel confined and helpless- or it can cause anger and resentment at an unjust, impossible situation. Mindfucks can be a terrifying, exhilarating ride into helplessness – or a furious, potentially disastrous event. Know what you want, know what you *are likely to get*, and plan it out.

I just want to say again: Remember that the goal is the *state of mind invoked in the subject, not the sequence itself*. If you have fetishized a specific sequence in your head, i.e. "First I'll get some guys to follow him a few blocks, so he's really nervous, then I'll jump out in the duck suit..." then you are not thinking about your subject, and will need to find a subject to suit your fantasy, not a scenario to mindfuck your subject. In a Mindfuck, it's about the *subject*, not the sequence. Know what you want your subject to *experience*, as opposed to what you want to *do* to them. Your focus is on achieving the *goal state*.

Know yourself

Never threaten anything you are not willing or capable of doing.

There is nothing more disempowering than an empty threat.

If your subject knows you, they will know when you are bluffing. Even if they don't, they may well call your bluff. The answer: Don't bluff. *Ever.* I'm sure you can come up with suitably dismaying threats and dire promises – especially if you know what some of those negative reinforcement buttons are. As a rule, I advise against any form of outright lie in a mindfuck scenario, it simply devolves to role-playing or worse, broken trust. However, the pressure to find just the right thing to say can lead you to saying foolish things if you are not careful. Don't bluff – it might give them something to hang on to, and we would not want that.

Avoid lying, allow misconception

In the same vein, I will always advise avoidance of the deliberate falsehood. Not only can you damage your relationship and the essential trust, you can get *caught*. It's a bad moment for Oz the Great and Terrible when that pesky dog runs behind the curtain. If a falsehood is absolutely necessary, make certain that it is one that is resolved *in the positive*, on the side of safety and/or structure. For example, if you need to convince your slave that you will be away for the night (in order to have a staged abduction occur), and have no other option but to lie, at least in the end it will turn out that you were there. Making sure all went well... easily forgivable. Consider the inverse – promising you'll be somewhere, and failing to show up – a much more upsetting situation. Of course, there's the third alternative – promise you'll be there, *appear* that you have failed to show, then turn up at the end to show that you *were* there, and *were* managing the situation... thus, actually remaining true to your word. The *appearance* of dishonesty is an acceptable tool, provided you turn out to be dependable in the end.

Never compromise your structure

The last of the honesty issues I am going to expand on is the structure of your relationship. A Mindfuck is no excuse to break agreed limits, to suddenly and abruptly introduce un-negotiated elements, or to force issues of contention. Nor is it an acceptable substitute for therapy – leave the psychodrama to the experts. Look at your structure honestly for what it is, and stay inside that framework in your actual deeds, if not the appearance of those deeds. Earlier I mentioned a boy who is phobic of cockroaches; we can safely assume that they are mentioned among his limits somewhere. It is inappropriate, therefore, to actually unleash a Madagascar hissing roach into his cage, or possibly to even bring it into the room with him. However, if you have spent a week leaving evidence that suggests you *might* have ordered some, and then make some scratchy scampering motions across his chest with a feather while you make sounds of amused disgust while he is blindfolded... that's all well within the structure. The roaches are only in his imagination.

Conspire with those you trust

If you want a mystery package to show up at your door, it's a little awkward to send it from the home you both share. Why go to the sitcom-like trouble, when you can have a co-conspirator mail it? If you want your slave with modesty issues to worry about a peeping tom, you are only going to be able to go out and rattle the bushes by the window so many times before your boy puts it together – it would be his first thought, anyway. Have a friend do it the first night... that will firmly establish an unknown third party, so when you start leaving scary (but really hot) letters pasted together out of magazine letters and scraps of dirty magazines, the illusion is already in motion. Besides, if your friends are twisted enough to help you, they're twisted enough to have some good ideas you might not have thought of. Don't just enlist Dominants, either – there are few things most submissives like more than seeing one of their own suffer.

Take advantage of situations of leverage

Improvise. Adapt, adopt, improve. Think fast, wabbit. Your opportunities to sink the screws in a little deeper are coming all the time. If possible, don't pursue them – let them come to you. Letting her think you sent away for a dental drill on eBay is a lot more convincing if she brings up a related subject and you infer it, rather than a clumsy attempt to steer the conversation. Take your time, gather your information, and act when the opportunity arises.

Creating your Sequence

ILLUSIONS

Everyone believes evidence; especially the evidence of their own eyes. To create an *illusion* is to provide that evidence. Let's say you've threatened your slave with moving her out to an all-weather dog kennel in the backyard. She's terrified. You don't have to mention it again – why would you, when you can simply order supply catalogs from pet stores, leaving them around book-marked to kennels? One or two over a two week period would do. Then leave one out with a circled cage, and the order form ripped out. When she asks about it, simply reclaim the catalogs and blandly deny that you ordered anything.

The idea of an illusion is to allow your subject to jump to the conclusions you have led him to. People are more convinced by what they *decide* than by what they are told. A few small pieces of leading evidence – carelessly left about or clumsily concealed – are worth hours of threats and innuendo. People are all talk; evidence suggests *action*. What's worse is that this is action that is *already underway*.

PROPS

The foundation of *illusion* is the *prop*, the "leading evidence" that brings the subject to the desired conclusion. Unexplained packages or visits, mail order catalogs, letters written in a strange hand or from unknown email addresses... a fake website. These things are easily created or obtained, and are powerfully convincing. It seems to me that the most convincing way to use such "evidence" is to let it be discovered, rather than present it directly. Perhaps a third party co-conspirator can bring it to light?

"So, Sue... did your Sir get it yet?"

"Get what?"

"Oh – my Sir was talking to your Sir – He said your Sir was going to make some big purchase. Some sort of all-weather dog kennel?"

"What?"

"Yeah – He showed Him the catalog... I have it right here..."

"Oh, my God..."

Denial and creation of information/sensory input

Plausible deniability.

Nothing will convince someone of something faster than the sense that something is being kept from him or her. Something *vital*. Say you want to convince her that you *did* receive an all-weather dog kennel, and she'll be sleeping there from now on.

You left catalogs. She found them. She's worried. When she asks, what do you do? Tell the truth:

"No, I did not buy a kennel."

"Do you promise?"

"Why should I have to? I just told you I didn't. That's enough for you. We are not talking about this again."

Your goals are achieved: You have led her to a conclusion, you have told her the absolute truth, and you are well within your structural guidelines. Later on, after she's found the empty cardboard box (which you engineered a label for on your PC and had a friend send you) out back, cuff her in the corner and blindfold her while you hammer *something* together in the backyard. What she does not know is what she will be most afraid of.

DENY FACTS, CREATE INNUENDO

You are having a surprise party for your slave… but you want to convince her that she is being delivered into the hands of brutal, uncaring "professionals" for "retraining." A faked website is good – a phone conversation she can eavesdrop on is better. Talk to a few friends about the idea; take notes on possible "locations." If you build a website, give her that one and a list of similar sites to research for you. Refuse to discuss it – you "have not made up your mind," you are "waiting to see if she improves." When you finally load her terrified carcass into the car, make her pack a suitcase with a few (very few) regimented things. Blindfold her, and off you go, to drive around for two hours while your friends arrange the party back home. Better yet, blindfold her, toss her shackled ass into a strange car, and have a friend (who will *not* speak to her) drive her around while *you* set up the surprise.

SUGGESTIONS

Applying context is the heart of suggestion. While illusion is primarily visual or material (use of props, etc.), suggestion is primarily verbal or written. The offhanded comment, the dire threat, or the innocent expressions of interest are all good examples. How these things are used is a matter of craft, combining elements of *repetition* and *insinuation*.

REPETITION

Say it once – it won't stick. Say it too many times, and you are obviously "up to something." It's a delicate balance. You should know your people, but in general I find that three times over a week is just enough to get their alarm bells to go off, but not enough to be obvious. You want to plant a suspicion, a doubt – you want to inspire *dread*.

The Forked Tongue

If you want to actually do the research, pick a more innocent topic and see how many repetitions it takes until they look at you and go, *"What's with you and sunflowers this week, Sir?"* Then, when you are starting your mindfuck, aim for one or two less repetitions. Remember, topics they are afraid of/fascinated with/ excited by will stick faster than your "sunflower" experiment.

INSINUATION

There is a screenwriting phrase: *"The scene is never about what the scene is about."*

Whenever possible, do not address the suggestion directly to your subject. Talk about a scene in a movie – once it's brought up, talk about other elements of the film. (You can't really talk about *Deliverance* without talking about the "squeal like a pig" scene – but you are talking about a movie – not anal rape. Really. Honest.) Bring your suggestion up as *tangential* to the actual focus of the dialog. Ideally, you want to be able to look back and say "I mentioned X during our conversation *about* Y."

When you combine this with an awareness of your opportunities, you'll end up with a situation where something gets mentioned four or five times over a span of a conversation, an afternoon or a week – yet it's utterly blameless. *Plausible Deniability*. This amounts to an application of the power of suggestion. If you engage someone in a conversation about Chinese food, and use the phrase Chinese food over and over, constantly mentioning Chinese food and how much you like Chinese food, and then ask them:

"What do you want to eat?"

What was *your* first thought?

You don't have to mean it, you don't have to really want it, but what was the very first thing that crossed your mind?

All you want to do is make them *think* it. Once you've done that, you are well on your way.

Our example this time – a Goddess is going to give her boy to a Dominant leatherman of her acquaintance... or so she wants him to think. In truth, it's just going to be her with a strap-on again... but she wants to fuck his mind, along with the rest of him. For a week or so beforehand she begins dropping comments.

Offhanded comment

For example, talking about things that turn him on, so the conversation turns to the sounds a lover makes;

> "You sound great when I fuck you – I just wish I could see you better... I want to watch you get fucked someday."

(Our boy is enthusiastic – he assumes she means by another Dominant Woman. Let him think so for now.)

The conversation can now turn to *other* sights that turn them on, and the seed is planted.

Dire Threats

> "Maybe you'd think a little clearer if you appreciate how good I am to you – I know a leatherman who would be happy to teach you a lesson... right up your ass, boy."

(Especially in context, this is not going to inspire the enthusiasm of the first comment... but the seed has been planted.)

If he tries to react to that, bring his attention back to the subject – the reason that you are threatening him in the first place, what he's done wrong. That's what you are talking about, after all.

INNOCENT EXPRESSION OF INTEREST (INSINUATION):
> *"I think Tom of Finland art is really hot – I always wanted to watch men fuck each other."*

From here you can go on to art, gay porn, or other related subjects.

Individually, each one of these may have some effect – but what if you strung them together over the course of a week? We'll get back to this example a little later, to suggest how to tie all your hard work together.

DREAD

Almost universally, Mindplay is about creating fear, dread, and tension in your subject. Not by definition – I mean, you could use all these techniques to make your subject think you are having eggs for breakfast and then "*Surprise! We're having cereal!*" Tell me if it's any fun. Me – I'm all for deep hurting, so that's what we'll talk about.

Fear and *dread* enhance the sensation of being controlled, of one's fate not being in one's own hands... which is what submissives are there for, after all. Like a roller coaster, fear is the purest experience of loss of control, the mainline rush for the sensation junkie. Fear, however, is fleeting. People cannot really maintain states of terror very long – most people shut down, or enter alternate states of consciousness. So – save that for last.

What you are most often looking for is *dread*, the evil twin of anticipation. Dread can exist in varying levels throughout the experience, and can be maintained almost indefinitely to some degree. Where fear is the immediate reaction to a perceived threat, dread is stomach aching, lingering trepidation – especially of the unknown. When mixed with a fetish context, it makes for a memorable waiting period as the inexorable drama of the Mindplay unfolds.

DENY INFORMATION

The most useful way to create *dread* is to deny information. Strange sounds, closed doors, and secrecy are all tools to create fear of the unknown. As a rule, an unknown is always scarier than what is known, no matter how terrible that knowledge. Pain can be endured, humiliations braved, challenges overcome – but there is no getting around a mystery. Especially, an oh-so-*terrible* one.

INNUENDO

Never commit to anything, admit nothing, and don't give a scrap away more than you have to. However – you have to find ways to reference the idea you are trying to inspire dread of. Reading a book or watching a movie – conspicuously – that features a scene known to have the element in question will often bring the idea to mind in your subject. Refer to these things obliquely. *Insinuate.* Give the impression that it's on your mind – but never clearly own up to it. Never commit to your illusion until it's too late for them to stop or avoid what they fear is going to happen.

PUTTING IT ALL TOGETHER

In all of the examples I have provided so far, there has been some element of dread and the denial of information, the insinuation of the source of fear, and the illusion of the fear. Let's look at them:

Boy terrified of cockroaches

Denial: He never sees any roaches. (There are none.) He is never told you *did* obtain roaches for certain. (You didn't).

The Forked Tongue

Insinuation: You mention that it's possible to order huge roaches online ... more than once.

Illusion: An empty package, a stiff feather across the skin, and the hissing sound from a small spray can of compressed air.

Modest slave/ Peeping Tom

Denial: The slave never sees who is out there for certain (it's you or an accomplice), the letters have no postage or identifying marks.

Insinuation: You mention a stranger standing by the front walk a few days running, or telephone hang-ups (while the slave was not at home).

Illusion: You arrange for a friend to be visible (briefly) outside the window, leave cryptic messages in the mailbox, and arrange phone hang-ups when you are *both* home.

Slavegirl/ dog kennel

Denial: She is told that there is no kennel. She is given no further information, and the issue is conspicuously *never* discussed. When you are "building" the kennel in the backyard, she is blindfolded or otherwise unable to see what you are doing.

Insinuation: You threaten it once, and drop statements about the idea into other conversations, seeding her consciousness.

Illusion: A curious box, pet catalogs ... and finally, the sound of construction in the backyard while she is helpless to observe or interfere.

Slavegirl/ surprise party

Denial: She is told that you are considering sending her away, and you never give her a definite answer. When she is packed into a car without discussion or notice, she is blindfolded and wondering which one of the "institutes of training" she has been researching she'll be sent to – and the driver will not answer any questions.

Insinuation: Sending her to do research on the institutes in question, surfing websites and gathering information

Illusion: A faux website specializing in all the things she is most afraid of, a nightmare of a "training facility," a mysterious driver in a strange car, a long ride to nowhere.

Boy to be fucked by leatherman

Denial: It is never discussed or brought up for negotiation of any sort, blindfolding at the moment of truth.

Insinuation: References to gay porn, leathermen you know, erotic art of the right type, *Deliverance*...

Illusion: Phone calls from an unidentified man, a man present at the final hour (or you in heavy boots, smoking a cigar while he's blindfolded), large gloves, and a new and unfamiliar strap-on.

Once you have it all... where do you go from here? What's the payoff?

The Final Act

Give the people what they want.

A good mindfuck ends with a spike point – a moment of decision or conflict that brings all the factors to a peak; essentially, a final act. It is the heart of the Mindfuck, the payoff – and allows closure, a relief of the dread

The Forked Tongue

and tension that you have been carefully cultivating for hours, days, weeks, or even months.

In some ways, this is the easiest part – it's the moment you probably first envisioned. I'll run a few examples by you, but what I really want to address is *why*, and what you might expect to happen.

The end of a mindplay allows for an explosion of fear or other mental state – but it also allows a catharsis, a moment where after the world has been turned upside-down, it rights itself. This is the moment that reaffirms trust, commitment, and structure. However, it does not always come immediately. There can be periods of shock and uncertainty as the subject tries to realign a reality which has been drastically and intentionally altered, and he or she may need multiple reassurances that this is not yet another trick. Give it, allowing them to get their bearings, so your work can be appreciated from a place of security and stability. *Guide them to the goal state by what you say, how you make them feel.*

Just a note – if it seems like it's going wrong, if their panic has the wrong taste or seems violent or beyond what you wanted from the experience – don't be proud. Call it off, let them in on it, and calm them down. Find out what went wrong.

That way, you'll know what to do *next* time to get what you want.

Boy terrified of cockroaches

Simple enough – after you've had enough, just remove the blindfold, showing him the feather and the spray can. He'll get it.

Modest slave/ Peeping Tom

Arrange a ringing of the doorbell while he is tied and blindfolded, and then wait a few minutes. When you come back, wear heavier shoes, alter your tread, and wear gloves. Whisper that he is "just like you pictured him;" even better, get an accomplice to do it. If you don't smoke, light a cigarette. Rather than continue the scene as usual, explore his body like it's new to you, increasing in roughness until you get him right where you want him... then, at the end, let him see you.

Slavegirl/ dog kennel

Once she thinks that the kennel is built in the back yard, lead her out blindfolded. Make her recommit to your authority, reaffirming, in her own words, that you have the right to do this if you want. Make her admit it, even ask for it. Inexpensive large pet carriers or doghouses are available at pet stores – crawl her in, lock her down, and give it a few minutes – especially if she thinks you have walked away. When you've had enough, give her back her sight – and bring her back inside, so she can reclaim the place in your space that you have allowed her – most likely with an all new appreciation for your generosity.

Slavegirl/ surprise party

This one ends pretty classically, with the guests yelling "surprise" and your subject blinking and staring. The positive effect of a lot of people there with smiles will put her back on her feet quickly.

Boy to be fucked by leatherman

When you are done, take the blindfold/hood off so he can see who it is violating him. Again, pretty classic... of course, you could keep him in suspense a while – then walk into the room wearing the boots, gloves, strap on and smoking the cigar. Your call.

The important common denominator here is the return to normality, the closure – allowing the mindplay to end. This allows your subjects to regain their equilibrium, and they will probably experience a massive high, as well as allowing you to take your bows.

Pushing the Envelope

If you feel really confident about where you are, where you are heading, and what you want to happen, if you are there but not-quite-over, then you want to debate pushing the envelope:

> Get the boy to admit that he'd brave the cockroaches for his Sir.
>
> Get sexual in the scene with the slave who thinks you are a stalker.
>
> Keep the slavegirl in the dog kennel overnight.
>
> Subject the birthday girl to a degrading inspection at the hands of unknown strangers before taking the blindfold off and yelling "Surprise" – in the same room.
>
> Try to make the boy come and admit excitement while being fucked by the mystery "Leatherman."

I will not sanction going the extra mile as mandatory, or even desired. I will not commit on paper to saying that it's a good idea. I will, however, say that under the right circumstances with the right people, it is everything it is supposed to be. Be careful, people, and don't be stupid. If you are going to do something, do it right. Sometimes, you just have to say: *"Go big or go home."*

The Cattle Prod Example

I am going to assemble one more example, step by step; trying to incorporate every principle we've talked about:

> A. Buy catalog, leave available (Illusion – prop)

B. Talk about cattle prod in conversation (Suggestion/insinuation/innuendo)
C. Remove catalog (Dread – denial of information)
D. Determine that the prod is within structure (Dread – insinuation, Suggestion)
E. Make wrapper or unmarked box visible (Dread, Illusion – props, denial of information, leading to conclusion)
F. Create deciding moment, moment of conflict. Sensory dep is VERY useful in many cases.
G. Push the envelope ("Stick out your tongue.")
H. Joy buzzer, alarm clock, kiss, or shock – (Resolution)
   Be certain to create the goal state with commentary, criticism, or praise. (Payoff)
I. Follow up – one of these days, get the prod.

One final note – Every so often, I advise you to carry through on your threats. Pose a threat you are willing to go through with, and follow up on it if required. Make it real, make it happen. Every outlandish thing you do gives credibility to a dozen Mindfucks. If they think that your threat is simply beyond you, they'll learn very quickly not to believe it – and, I suspect, will be more than a little disappointed in the end. But if they think you are capable of *anything*...

Then they'll <u>believe</u> anything.

I started with mindfucks for a specific reason: to take the focus off of the physical, the traditional "whips and chains" idea, while still incorporating the physical and material. Everything we discuss in this book is unified by one continuing theme... altering the mental state of your subject. We will slowly begin including more and more physical elements as we go on, incorporating them as needed to create deeper and deeper states, getting our hands further and further into the heads of those under us.

Now, you can look at the mindfucks idea as a complete, if somewhat complex and perhaps overwhelming, scenario. It is actually an ordered collection of *individual tools*. Let's say you want to throw together a mindfuck but don't want to work on it for weeks – get ahold of one or two simple props and wing it. You want to make your subject worry that you are a serial killer for the evening? A shrine of cut up photos and a few candles makes people very uneasy, as would jagged lipstick marks on the mirror. "Poof" – instant psychopath, especially if they've never been to your place before. Want to suggest a social or political menace? Klan and Nazi pamphlets and paraphernalia are easily available on the internet, and eBay can keep you off distasteful mailing lists while you are at it.

The point is that any of these tools are useful on their own, not just when arranged in a more complex sequence. Of course, the bigger you go, the more profound the impact.

CHAPTER 4: HUMILIATION
Nothing Cuts Like Words

This is a tough one.

Unlike many other chapters of this book, there is not a lot of science here, not a lot of hard facts and procedures to fall back on. Interrogation, hypnosis – many of our subjects are well documented, and all it takes is an attempt to present them in a different light, breaking them down into easy-to-handle tools. In addition, there are reputable sources to seek out expertise. Not so here.

Humiliation is so intensely personal, so profoundly subjective by its very nature, that there are very few universal guidelines to present. The best we can do is subdivide, to identify ideas, notions and trends so that as you work on deciphering the complex code of your subject's nature, you have some guidelines that might help. These observations are general and sweeping at best; the real challenge will always lie with you in finding the buttons to push, the soft spots to probe and lay open.

The first of the hurdles are your own preconceptions and fantasies. To understand your subject, these must be put aside (for the time being). If you are filtering all the information through your own desires, you are not seeing anything accurately; the lens you are looking through is masked by your own reflection. (Don't worry – we'll get back to your desires. They are what is really important here, after all.) So to begin, take note of what your own ideas and desires *are*. Are there words or images that move you? Crawling, crying, begging? Public exposure? Specific outfits, gear, or required nudity? Know yourself; know what you want – so you can identify these concepts if they intrude. By the way – all the following suggestions for figuring out what makes your subject tick are just as applicable for figuring out your own kinks... which can be an invaluable tool for getting what you want and need.

What you are looking for are common threads, themes that run through your subjects' fantasies and desires. In trying to discuss these things, you are likely to run into the first obstacle – *discussing them at all*. In my experience, hardcore fetishists will have no problem sharing their objectives in my experience; often the problem is getting them to *stop* talking about them. But others are far more likely to be shy and/or guilty about their desires. We spend our entire lives covering over and armoring our vulnerabilities, that's a lifetime of conditioning to overcome. I have often encountered the idea that "It's no good if I have to tell/ask him to do it." Essentially, the desire of the submissive (and often the Dominant) is that the partner in question wants "it" on their own, for themselves, that it be a shared craving. Such a perfect organic match is profoundly rare. The problem is, silently wishing won't help. Most infuriating of all is the "I don't want to tell you, just *do it to me!*" thing, which seems to rely on your amazing psychic powers to fathom their needs – and if you don't, it's *your fault*. Sometimes, it's enough to make you want to hang up your leathers entirely.

So – if you can't depend on someone to simply spill their innermost, deepest secrets and shameful desires, what can you do?

You can *pay attention*.

Look for "tells." A *tell* is the poker term for the involuntary giveaway through which players reveal when they are nervous, excited, or bluffing. Blushing, widened pupils or averted eyes, involuntary hesitation, stammering or losing their train of thought, non-sequiturs or abrupt changes in topic, shifts in body language – all of these can be revealing signals that you have hit upon something. The fact is that on some level they *want* to tell you, (or at least, they want you to know). They are just too conflicted to do so easily. So, look for signals. But seeing as the stimulus for such tells is not always something you want to bring up directly, it's often best to use indirect stimulus, much as we touched on in the mindfucks chapter. Expose them to scenes or media with some of the elements in question running through them, an innocent conversation about something else that touches on the concepts, or most underhanded of all, start slipping it in dirty talk during sexual or scene situations. People are often very open when drunk or in the sack; but do keep in mind, the things which come out of a groaning partner during sex (or any altered state) are often *not to be taken literally*. A moaning, eye-rolling confession of wanting to be brutally sodomized with a Louisville slugger on home plate of Wrigley Field in front of a capacity crowd may be hot in the moment, but is as unlikely as it is infeasible. The keys here (for example) are the *threads*: sodomy and/or public exposure. Note them, and see if they repeat other ways in other revelations. (On the other hand, if Wrigley Field keeps coming up, it may be a fetish – which is another matter entirely.)

There are a few different concepts which we'll be working with here, and as usual, clarity is paramount. There are three closely related concepts at hand: Humiliation, Degradation, and Objectification. Though subtle, the differentiations are important. Keep in mind, there is a lot of overlap, and these distinctions are primarily for the purposes of discussion.

hu•mil•i•ate (hyoo-mil-ee-eyt) **(Humiliation)**
tr.v. **hu•mil•i•at•ed, hu•mil•i•at•ing, hu•mil•i•ates**

To lower the pride, dignity, or self-respect of.

"You filthy piece of shit."

"Touch you? You must be joking. I don't even want to look at you."

The Forked Tongue

> *"Tell me what a worm you are…"*

Therefore, this is personal. It's about **who someone *is*** by *assigning* values, attributes, and descriptors. (Shit, unworthiness/ugliness, worm.)

ob•jec•ti•fy (uhb-**jek**-tuh-fahy) **(Objectification)**
tr.v. **ob•jec•ti•fied, ob•jec•ti•fy•ing, ob•jec•ti•fies**

To present or regard as an object: "Because we have objectified animals, we are able to treat them impersonally."

> *"Animals don't sleep on the bed – they sleep on the floor. So, as long as you are my animal, will you too."*

> *"Shut it. You stand right there until I need you, and when I'm done, you go right the fuck back. No talking."*

> *"It puts the lotion on its skin or else it gets the hose again."* (Sorry – just wanted to see if you were still paying attention. But come on, you can't tell me you did not think that was a *little* hot. C'mon.)

So this is by definition, *impersonal* – it is about **who or what they are *not***. (Animals sleep on the floor vs. people, who sleep on the bed. Reduction to use as a utility – being defined by one's *function*, referred to/treated as an object – "it.")

de•grade (di-**greyd**) **(Degradation)**

1. To reduce in grade, rank, or status; demote.

2. To lower in dignity; dishonor or disgrace: a scandal that degraded the participants.

3. To lower in moral or intellectual character; debase.

4. To reduce in worth or value: degrade a currency.

> *"Crawl… show me you know your place."*

"You'll have to excuse her – she's just that stupid."

"If you were any kind of a man, you'd stand up for yourself... But you like this, don't you?"

This does not address who or what they are, it **belittles the *quality or value* of the subject**, their *worth*. (Reduction of social standing – "place." Denigration of intellect – "stupid." Denigration of masculinity.)

As you can see, there is a lot of gray area, and in reality the lines are blurred; the definitions are not so convenient. So why break it down at all?

Now, about what to **do** with our newfound knowledge...

Nothing cuts like words.

Words assign *context* – almost everything we do is defined by what we say and how we say it. Words can give actions weight and meaning well beyond the physical, or they can render actions superfluous. They are the means to mar what a whip can never reach – the *self*. In everything we explore in this chapter – and, come to think of it, every other chapter as well – we frame and aim our actions with what we say. So we will start with this unifying element, and use it to carry us through the facets of the topic. Verbal abuse is both a science and an art. As usual, the first question is: *What result do I want?* First, we look at what creates the desired state in your subject – what are the core kink threads? What *works*?

To do this, we have to figure out what gets the right reactions – namely, the reactions you want – from your subject. Nothing here is universal. One subject may get a charge out of name calling and cruelty because she feels it's safe – not real, almost intimate; another would laugh at such matters because certain words don't cut, they are safe – too safe for her. A third might not feel anything from negative attention at all – it is dismissal and being ignored that really gets to him. Knowing these differences, and having the common language to discuss them, is integral to our purpose here. I knew a lovely redhead who loved being called a "stupid cow." She was very smart and very attractive; thus these words were bloodless, safe, *hot* – intimacies. It would be even more effective publicly; her Sir was quite gifted with vicious name-calling and not at all afraid to do so in public for best effect. She was into what we are calling humiliation; the common thread in her case is that the denigration is assigned – it is a value which is designated by the superior, but not rooted in fact. I know another woman who would find such things silly. She needs to be hit where it actually *does* hurt: the masochistic joy for her is the twisting of the knife and exposure of her actual insecurities, and anything bloodless is a waste of time. My animal is one of the smartest people I know, but there is no joy in being called "stupid" for her, those would just be fightin' words. Not the reaction I want. Instead, it is denigrating her social position, her place (with me) which takes the hit and provokes the proper reaction. I'd refer to the latter two examples as degradation – the lessening and belittling of what is actually there. Lastly is objectification – this is the dismissal of the subject as a person entirely, reducing them to a function or an object. Using someone as a cupholder, thankless labor, selfish sexual use, dismissive behavior – all of these things can be considered objectification of one sort or another. A young woman I played with for a time cracked and melted when I renamed her "nothing;" reinforcing it with leading questions: "What does your opinion amount to?" "Nothing, Sir." "What do your feelings on this matter have to do with anything?" "Nothing, Sir."

Let's start with the basics: Manners (and the lack of them).

One of the most elemental ways of demonstrating social inequality is *manners*. The elemental good manners that (one hopes) our parents taught us are the primary social mechanism for demonstrating respect for our peers and deference to our superiors. Although it is looked down on in polite society to be actively rude to our subordinates, they may not receive the same courtesies our peers do. Even in the USA, where most formality has dissolved into the melting pot in our endless quest to seek "equality," certain boundaries still exist. You call the judge "Your Honor," you call your boss "Mr./Ms. Whoever" (at least until they tell you otherwise), the same goes for teachers and business associates. If you don't know the waitress's name, you are still more likely to say, "Excuse me, Miss?" than "Hey, you!" or, even worse, to snap your fingers to get her attention.

The people who serve you are under you because they do not want to be treated like everyone else; on certain levels they do not want to be a peer. How that difference manifests successfully varies from structure to structure. For some, the alteration or eradication of civil niceties is both an intimacy and a reminder of station. This can go well beyond the mere elimination of your "please" and "thank you," although the effectiveness of such things is not to be underestimated. (Nor is the effect such brusqueness can have on bystanders. People can jump to some pretty unpleasant conclusions, even in scene-friendly situations, when their sense of propriety is challenged.)

But the question of public or private is not just a question of social appropriateness and consequence; it's also a thread that is important to pick up on. The context of an action is framed not only by words, but by circumstance; and public/private is a near universal consideration. The servant who would greedily eat dinner from a bowl at your feet in private may react in a totally different way if it is demanded in public, even if it's been done a hundred times before at home. An action which has little fetish value in private may have a profound impact in a public setting. People are often perfectly comfortable with nudity or revealing clothing in the privacy of their own home, but being paraded in such a fashion before strangers can be a very different matter. Often just the introduction of witnesses can turn a nearly insignificant or commonplace gesture into a profound event.

The Forked Tongue

While doing your homework, listen for the cues about the context. Be keenly aware of the power of public exposure – especially in terms of humiliation, degradation, and objectification – to cause your efforts to crash and burn horribly or perhaps to be *profound*, in every sense of the word.

Humiliating your subject through assigning values – name calling – is one form of verbal abuse. It takes a vivid imagination and an ease with words to be really good, and at the very least one should be inventive (and vicious) enough to keep from sounding like a broken record. However, calling your favorite people sissies, bootlickers and worms is far from the end-all of this particular entertainment. Degradation – being cruelly critical of their actual abilities – has its own merits. Where name-calling stings and shames, degradation may cut a bit deeper, as you are addressing real qualities, and finding them lacking. Some people are impervious to this sort of thing – they are confident in their own capabilities, and criticism rolls off them without a mark or a thought. However, such people are rare, and I have found that everyone is insecure about something, or better yet, knows they are lacking in one department or another. Other people are walking targets to any real or imagined slight to their abilities, often finding fault in themselves where none exists. Not only do you want to know where on this spectrum your subject falls, and regarding what topics, you want to understand what effect such treatment will have on them, and if that effect is the one you are seeking. I differentiate between degradation and humiliation this way because people's reactions to these stimuli can often vary wildly, and on the surface it can be baffling trying to determine what set off the reaction in question. Every subject is different.

The third concept at hand is not about what kind of negative attention you pay. Objectification – at least on the surface – is about *not paying attention at all*. This is an illusion; it takes just as much focus as any of the others, often with the added challenge of appearing *not* to be doing that very thing. Part of the secret is the inherent contradiction. Very few people actually want to be ignored in any real way. For most, objectification is the *illusion* of being ignored in some fashion, maintained by altering the traditional forms of attention. Now, I am not addressing the bondage bottom who wants to be tied up and then "left alone" to struggle in his or her own world; that's not objectification precisely because of the lack of interaction. Objectification means ignoring the subject *as a person* in some fashion. The most common fantasy seems to be being reduced to a sexual plaything, to be *defined by that purpose* and have the needs and feelings of a peer and a person "ignored."

The verbal element of this can be addressed by things such as changing pronouns (he/she/you) to "it," not addressing the subject directly, or talking to others as if the subject were not present, and/or by resisting the temptation to interact with the subject *for anything other than the stated purpose*. That can be difficult; love, familiarity, or discomfort with acting in such a fashion can often make it feel unnatural or isolated for the top.

The other thing that can make such a thing difficult is the fact that it's rare that the subject actually wants to be ignored; what most of them want is to be interacted with *differently*. Take for example the subject who wants to be treated like an object or furniture (fornophilia). They still want to be the footstool or cup holder *of the Superior*, to be in the same room, to interact in a limited fashion dictated by their function – but still, to *interact*.

Physical aids are incredibly useful to push those buttons. Reducing someone to a cup holder while you read, hold a conversation with a peer, or even sleep. Hoods used to steal his or her face, can obscure both their and your sense of them as an individual. (It's a powerful psychological change, not just for the hooded servant but for the superior as well – we respond sympathetically to faces, and likewise respond to their absence.) Personally, I tend to usurp all gender privilege – I have all the privilege of a male in our culture – but my servants hold doors, chairs and coats for me, take me to dinner, buy me flowers – all privilege is, by definition, *mine*. These are things you can *take*, and that's what objectification is – taking away.

Another approach to achieve a similar effect is taking your subject for granted, the hybrid child of degradation and objectification. No please, no thank-you, no acknowledgement of effort, performance, or merit; a simple expectation of compliance and performance, a foregone conclusion. I have seen this reduce a servant to a needy, supplicating mass willing to crawl any distance for a crumb of recognition, and I have seen another walk from the Superior in disgust with his being such a self-centered jackass. Know your subject.

I wish I could give you one single, correct method – a sure-fire, foolproof, risk-free recipe for success. But, sadly, that's not gonna happen. As I said, there's no way to make this universal. What I can do is suggest different ways to look at things – essentially, do what I have been doing all along: suggest tools and leave you to build or burn as you see fit. We've talked about verbal tools, as the fundamental basics, that had to come first. Now we'll look at other options. This is by no means intended as an exhaustive list, just some ideas to suggest context.

Social

Humiliation
- *Public* derision and name calling
- Embarrassing or inappropriate clothing or demanded behavior

Degradation
- *Public* criticism of partner's abilities
- Obvious preference or favoritism of someone other than partner – flirting, dancing, etc.
- Taking over functions a partner would normally do for themselves

(or for you) due to "incompetence"

OBJECTIFICATION

- Employee functionality (for instance, while engaging partner as a driver, ride in the back, not holding any conversation)
- Dismissive interaction (ie: turning off a light when leaving a room the partner is still in)
- Discussing the subject with a peer as if the subject were not present

Physical

HUMILIATION

- Gaudy makeup (on either gender)
- Not being allowed to bathe, conversely being roughly scrubbed with a stiff brush for being "dirty"

DEGRADATION

- Eating from a bowl on the floor while you eat at a table
- Being denied silverware, or eating only your table scraps
- Sleeping on the floor or in a cage, being treated and kept as a pet or beast of burden

OBJECTIFICATION

- Serving as furniture or an object of decoration or utility
- Being summoned to perform a chore and then dismissed (from another room or across town)

PRACTICAL APPLICATION

This is really about observation. As you gather your data on what moves your subject in the directions you desire – or what moves him in directions you can adapt or adopt – look for commonalities, for common threads in the context of their desires. You are looking for a **core kink** – one drive that manifests itself in different ways. What do your subject's kinks have in common? Being dirty? Isolated? Afraid? An object, a second-class citizen, an owned possession?

If you can isolate that *core kink* – that one thread, which when plucked, resonates the way you want – you can begin to really experiment and give yourself a lot of room to play. If the resonating kink in your servant's mind is to feel violated (for example), you can improvise any number of amusing ways to bring that feeling about. We are not talking about **object fetish** – if your servant has a piss fetish, covering him in mud won't reach him at all... but if the core kink is *feeling dirty*, you can do any number of things – mud, piss, dirty laundry, hygiene restrictions, rubbing his face in spilled food, making him lick the bottom of your boots... improvise. You won't have to repeat yourself unless you want to. (A fetishist is different – it's all about *that one thing* – feet, for instance – and her whole world may revolve around that, sometimes to the exclusion of all else. There may be much less room for improvisation if your subject is **solely** a fetishist. However, just having a fetish – or more than one – does not mean that a servant is *limited* by that fetish; if it is just one element of their kink, then it's a valuable and exploitable resource.)

So it puts together something like this: you determine what *context* works best – objectification, degradation, and/or humiliation – and the *core kink* that you have reckoned links their twists together. Now you have a pretty well defined set of parameters within which you can consistently get the results you want; all from an abstract and often obfuscated set of desires even your subject may not really understand about himself. In **Chapter 5: Conditioning**, we will be exploring how applying a *framework* to encourage the redefinition and re-identification of your subject by defining their role in your service, possibly even down to his name, can help you bring about, recreate, maintain, and heighten the desired states you have initiated here.

MINEFIELDS AND MINDSETS

One of the trickier aspects to all this is the *minefield*. When exploring these things, one never knows when one will find something that goes "boom!" My first exposure to this was very early on for me, about twenty years ago or so. I was speaking to a young lady who was confessing fantasies of urinating on herself, in public or private... she went on at some length. When I ventured into what seemed to be a logical extension of the idea, my pissing on *her*, she flew into a rage and we were done talking. I felt, for all the world, like Elmer Fudd after his gun goes off in his own face... just blinking through the smoke, wondering *what the fuck just happened*. I know of a cross dresser – a very successful guy with the dominant women of my acquaintance, smart, well thought of, delights in various forms of humiliation – yet when a dominant woman I know did not want his opinion while they were doing chores and shopping together, he became deeply offended and walked out. Call one person "stupid" and they will follow you home, tail wagging, but another will slap your face and tell everyone what an ass you are. This is why I advocate a lot of research into a subject before getting too experimental with this stuff; the fact is (on this side of the leash), none of us like to lose. So, do your homework, study your subjects, and get to understand what makes them tick. *Play to win.*

The Forked Tongue

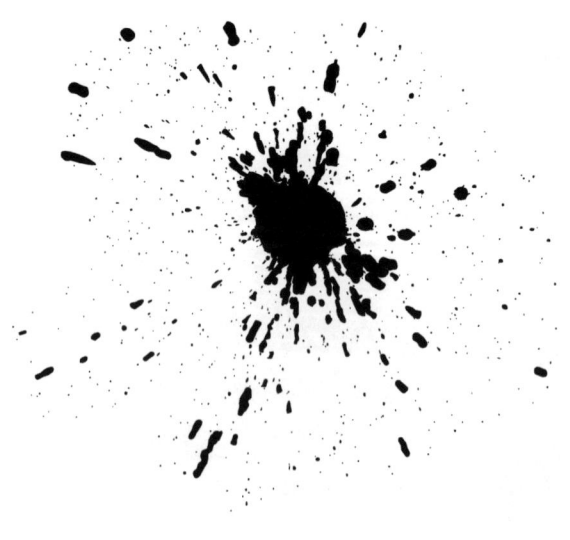

Chapter 5: Conditioning
The Hammer of the Mind

If the mindfuck is a bruise, then conditioning is a scar. Or perhaps more accurately, a tattoo.

As intense and visceral as a mindfuck may be, it has a beginning and an end. Like a bruise, it fades and disappears. It is *temporary*. In the end, the actors take their bows, the curtain falls, lights come up, and it is over; and everyone has a story to tell over cigarettes and coffee. Conditioning, however, is ongoing. It never ends. Different subjects and environments require a different intensity of maintenance to condition them, but the effort never really stops entirely. As a result, however, the curtain never really drops – the results are perpetual, often far outlasting the relationships that inspire them.

Conditioning takes many forms, and surrounds us constantly. Social conditioning is the forge that eventually turns us from greedy toddlers to (hopefully) giving, mature members of our society. And what defines the norm of any given society? Conditioning. On a personal level, that's what society is – how the individual is conditioned. As we narrow the focus, the more intense that conditioning becomes. Boarding and private schools increase the pressure of conditioning in specific directions, urban as opposed to suburban living and education narrow it further. The results begin to shine in a more polished, deliberate fashion in the military, where the science of conditioning is more intentionally, deliberately, and openly enforced. Narrow the focus further, increase the pressure and intensity, and you get the elite subdivisions: Marines, Army Rangers, and Green Berets. The lessons the military has to teach us are many and complex, tested and refined unrelentingly for centuries. If you want to know more about the science of conditioning in action, the first place I suggest you look is Army training manuals.

The more extreme the effects you seek to condition, the more work and maintenance you will need to exert, as conditioning does not stand in a vacuum. Any changes you achieve will be subject to the constant attrition of external stimuli such as environment, culture, and stress. In addition, there are the powerful factors of internal attrition due to emotional variance, personal history, and relationship status. In addition, some people are easier to condition than others. Some are very resistant, others imprint immediately. Given different types of stimulus or topic, these states can co-exist in the same person. Conditioning is a science, but its results are not uniform with every subject. However, given the intensity and consistency of the pressure applied, results are to some degree inevitable. Properly focused, conditioning works hand-in-hand with the most basic and elemental facets of human nature.

The science of behavioral conditioning is ancient and complex. It is an active, living field of study with elements of biology, sociology, psychiatry, and even physics, far too esoteric and complex for me to even proffer a professional or even a "qualified" opinion. Fortunately one does not need to be a physicist to drive a car. What we are going to address is a working knowledge of some techniques that tend to work, and are attainable without specialized laboratory conditions or equipment. Neither do I offer a complete program for a specific result, only methods and a layman's understanding of their application. As usual, I will offer you tools, but I will not tell you what to build.

Definitions:

Conditioning (noun): The process by which a subject comes to associate a desired response with a specific stimulus.

Reflex (noun): An automatic or involuntary response to a stimulus.

Response (noun): The reaction of an individual to a given situation or stimulus. This reaction can be internal as a series of thoughts or emotions or it can be physical in the form of a specific action. This response may or may not be automatic.

Training (verb): To accustom or condition to a mode of behavior or performance.

Discipline (noun): Training expected to produce a specific pattern of behavior, especially training aimed at moral or mental improvement. Alternately, "discipline" is used to refer to the result of such training.

Environmental acclimation: A constant reinforcement of the stimulus, with little or no direct action on the trainer's part on a moment-to-moment basis.

In broad strokes, we are going to talk about commonly sought-after results: reflexive responses, associative conditioning, positive/negative associations, pain/sexual conditioning, and overcoming previous conditioning. Taken together in our context, this could be considered "slave training,", although the exact same tools (for the most part) are forged in the military, the dojo, and many other crucibles that human culture has created.

Pain / Sexual Conditioning

The first and simplest application is *pain conditioning*. This tends to be the extent of "training" in most S/M circles, and it is often seen as a measure of a servant's value by those for whom physical kink is paramount. Pain conditioning takes, for the most part, only your enthusiasm and patience. In most cases, people will acclimate to a slowly escalating regimen of physical discomfort and endurance; marathon runners and weight lifters are everyday evidence. There is a sought-after goal, thus further and further exertions are demanded. Athletes have trainers to facilitate the process – an objective, disciplined (and hopefully knowledgeable) guide to encourage the athlete to push past his limits and reach his potential. Pain conditioning works similarly, and requires a similar motivation.

Sexual training is essentially similar to pain conditioning (and in some cases they are the same thing), with the added complication of not just inspiring drive, but hoping to inspire *enthusiasm*. This is not universal by any means, but can be an added complication when it is desired. Fortunately, we often have an added asset in these matters – sexual excitement. Many, many people are capable of amazing feats when excited that would be utterly beyond their endurance in a neutral or negative state.

Sexual excitement is too complex and contextual for me to be able to tell you how to create it at will as a dependent, automatic response. (If I could tell you that, I'd be doing it from my four hundred foot solid gold dirigible staffed with panting supermodels. That's the Holy Grail, that is.) But I can share some concepts that might be useful.

Orgasm Conditioning

Best trick in the world. It works best on multi-orgasmic women, and, sadly, it does not work on everybody universally – but what does? Deny orgasm to build up excitement, then use a simple statement to allow it to happen. *"Come for me."*, for example. Build up, withhold, repeat. In many cases you'll be able to get the orgasm on demand, first with little, then with no tactile stimulation. (Hypnosis can be a fine shortcut to the same effect, but I have heard from some that the conditioned orgasms are often more intense.) Basic conditioning at work – just use the same phrase, over and over, indelibly linking your command to her orgasm. Great fun at parties and crowded movie theatres. This is the basic lesson of conditioning.

ASSOCIATIVE SEXUAL CONDITIONING

We will be hitting on this topic again for other matters, but here it has a special focus. Decide what you want to associate – a perfume or cologne, a statement, a piece of music – and introduce it consistently and *quietly* during positive sexual and intimate experiences. I stress subtlety because the more consciously aware your subject is of the factor you are using, the more resistant to the conditioning they will become. If the data is logged on a subconscious level, it will become an *associated memory*, and eventually conditioned. If it is more conscious, it can be evaluated and rejected. So, rather than simply putting on a specific piece of music every time you give sexual attention, create a few mix tapes, *all* of which have that music on it *somewhere* – and time positive sexual attention to the timing of the music in question. Scent has a very strong connection to associative memory – a chosen perfume or cologne will always remind a partner of you – but if you wear a different scent for sexual encounters – *without drawing attention to this fact* – you may be able to eventually inspire sexual arousal simply by wearing it. Same goes for color, fabric, an item of apparel... the key to this is *subtlety*.

POSITIVE VS. NEGATIVE CONDITIONING

Now, authority exercised and obeyed is enough to allow the servant to comply, but there is an essential component missing there – *drive*. Without drive, the servant simply endures. With drive, the servant *strives*. To inspire drive is a simple matter of *frame-working* the presentation of the idea. A servant may obey – but to strive for more than mere obedience takes more interaction on the part of the superior in most cases. (We will be discussing frame-working further as one way to inspire drive when we discuss *redefinition*). Now, some bottoms are is already measuring themselves against past experience, striving to "do more" or "take more." This person is already motivated for pain conditioning – but what of those that are not?

The first and easiest motivator is *pride*. For the superior to express approval or even pride at their servant's endurance can be very powerful, especially if praise is used sparingly (more on that later). However, in most cases, it can only go so far by itself. I would suggest using the principles of re-identification in combination with spare praise: "*Master's dog would eat from the bowl. Are you your Master's dog? Do you want to be your Master's dog? Show me you want it. Prove to me that you are my dog.*" The alchemy in this combination is simple: In order to maintain a minimum standard by which to identify herself, she must reach your ever raising standards. To meet this ever climbing bar is not an occasion for praise every time, in fact it's the *least* they can do. To have it reasserted that they are, in fact, their Master's "X" will in *itself* become the prize.

Reflexes

Ideally, what conditioning seeks to create is an *involuntary response*. (We will be addressing more complex mechanisms later on.) You provide the stimulus, the body reacts. Conscious decision is removed from the equation; volition is not a factor. These responses in most cases cannot be created without *negative conditioning*. Orgasm is an exception, but really only circumstantially – orgasm being pleasurable is not only coincidental, it's an exception to the rules. Orgasm is a biological response to specific conditions, and the process described above can link those conditions to a stimulus of your choice. Pain is a similar process, only more immediate, more dependable and consistent, and therefore more effective.

Negative conditioning for a reflexive response is a matter of consistency, timing and repetition. If you wish to create a reflex, the recipe is simple: apply stimulus and immediately, if not sooner, apply a sudden negative reinforcement when the desired action is not forthcoming. If possible, this should all be in the same instant. It works in the dojo because everything happens *at once* – your opponent punches, you block properly or you get hurt. Repeat until the block becomes automatic, a reflex. It becomes even more powerful as the sensei drills the students in the blocks and katas, teaching the body to go on autopilot in their execution, then adds the repeated stimulus of the strike to be blocked. The sensei repeats this over and over again, until it happens reflexively, without thought. So, let's say you want to condition your servant to drop to his knees without a thought upon your barking the word "*Down*."

1. Repeat drills to master the proper position quickly and gracefully, at the command. Correct your servant's posture and form, and do not become lax in maintaining the standard you want. Work on this for a few weeks, regularly.

2. Step behind your servant, grab his hair and pull sharply downward while barking the command. Maintain the step one drills while occasionally, at unexpected times, performing the second step. If you are diligent in your application, soon your servant will drop into the correct posture without thought or hesitation upon command. It just takes work and diligence.

Repetition is as important as stimulus in this case. Repetition alone can train a marine to field strip and reassemble an M-16 blindfolded, especially coupled with the environmental pressures which are brought to bear (pride in self and company vs. shame before peers) – but that is not a *reflex*. Hitting the dirt while readying a weapon at the sound of a gunshot, rather than freezing in panic or scrambling chaotically – *that's* a reflex.

Positive conditioning is trickier, more akin to learning as a process than effective conditioning. It is also not supported by the same physical or psychological mechanisms as negative conditioning. When the body experiences negative stress – especially sudden pain – chemical processes in the brain are released to create a lasting aversion to it happening again. Positive reinforcement does not do the same thing. The brain has to learn to make those associations, and the older we are, the longer and less potent that process tends to be.

You can't develop a reflex action with a cookie.

Not only that, too many "cookies" are *counterproductive*. The more frequently and consistently they are offered, the more devalued the positive reinforcement becomes. In order to be sought after, such things must be both scarce and inconsistent. *Scarcity maintains value.* If the words *"good job"* are only heard at the very best of performance, they will be sought after; if they are heard after every completed task, they quickly become meaningless. The other factor is *Inconsistency*. It is true in both training humans and other animals (as many things are), that if the reward is forthcoming *every time* the "trick" in question is performed, performance will deteriorate the moment the reward is not present. Humans get the idea that they *deserve* reward, that it is their due, that it is supposed to happen – and if you do not produce the cookie they are expecting, you are not doing your job. It becomes **about the reward**.

If the rewards are inconsistent, they will be sought after. In animals, the performance of the action becomes associated with the *enthusiasm for the possibility*, not the reward itself. So it is with humans; thus inconsistency in these matters avoids the added, very human complications of *deserve, due,* and *supposed to*.

Associative Conditioning

Associative conditioning is not merely limited to sexual matters, it is in fact one of your most flexible tools. Nor is it only for positive reinforcement – it is actually easier to apply to negative conditioning, as are most conditioning matters. Like our previous example, all it requires is consistency and a degree of subtlety.

From your own life, you will doubtless be able to think of certain things which left an indelible impression on you: tones of voice of a displeased parent or mate, for instance. What we are discussing is simply causing those associations *intentionally*.

If you have a few close friends, or even better, an ex you are on good terms with, you can get a quick accounting of mannerisms and gestures you have that you might not even be aware of. (If any of these people are good mimics, this can be pretty amusing.) This will allow you the chance to develop some control of the signals you send, and to work to eliminate the ones you don't want and/or stress the ones you do. It takes a little work, and can even be awkward or embarrassing as you address your own habits – but it's well worth it. A controlled, self-aware presentation goes a long way. As you do this, you can begin to subtly stress certain phrases, tones or gestures with your subject. By way of example, I'll list a few of my own "tells" – the point is, however, that these are tells I am not only aware of, but have stressed to influence the behaviors of my servants:

Cracking the knuckles of my right fist while it hangs at my side

Translation: "You are pissing me off."

The tone and phrase of a sentence staring "Right... So...")

Translation: "Pay attention – you just made a big mistake."

A blank expression, slow and deliberate closing and opening of the eyes

Translation: "Shut up."

All of these set off alarm bells with people subject to my authority, and will usually cause an immediate cessation of whatever they are doing. Each of these gestures has different nuances and carries a different message and "tone," and I have deliberately cultivated the associations. I never *said* anything about it – that would be counterproductive. I let the associations form through experience.

Through simple deliberate and judicious application of your chosen stimulus, you can indelibly associate just about anything with just about anything else. Choose your context with care, because once the associations are made, they *stick*. Think of songs you hear that remind you of people, times, places, and relationships. Those associations may fade in intensity over time, but they will never go away completely.

MINDPLAY AND IDENTITY: REDEFINITION

More subtle than some of the games and ideas expressed above is the more long lasting concept of altering a servant's *sense of self*. I am not talking about crushing someone's self esteem, that's counterproductive and destructive on any long term basis. What I am talking about is the intimacy of *redefinition*.

The reason I use the word "servant" is twofold – first, it tends to be an accurate catch-all for the types of relationships I describe, and second because most other terms carry significant positive or negative baggage. How many debates have you observed over what a "true slave" is? How many people have you heard objecting to the word "subbie" or stating that one has to have some sort of certification to be called "Master?" Defining words have power. As far back as there have been people, there has been the idea that names have power – and it's still true. *Names are magic.*

In creating a structure, give careful regard to what the name of the servant's role is... boy, animal, slave, chattel, slut. What is this person in relation to you? Not who – *what* is she? And what is the *definition* of that role? Think about that: *You are redefining another person by the relationship they hold to you.* In effect, that makes *you* the central figure of their existence. You *define* them. Thus without you, they have no definition.

Now, this is not as simple as just saying so. It is part of an extended campaign to cement his definition of himself by your words. When I took on my boi, I spent a considerable amount of time framing my expectations not in simple "I want" terms, but by explaining what Flagg's Boy should do, should represent, what it *meant to be* Flagg's Boy.

All of these were standards to strive for, bars to meet, standards to bear, expectations to exceed. Because my Boy is a bio-female, seeking to understand masculinity from the inside out, I was in a unique position to rewrite existing or uncertain standards of good/bad, right/wrong, and pass/fail to be defined by my expectations and judgment of *his* actions. To be my Boy, these standards must be met. To fail continuously was to, in effect, not be my boy – to be nothing.

When I began my structure with my animal, I deliberately chose a term that had never been used with her (or to my knowledge, anyone) before. She had been in the service of another previously, and the term "slave" had been used casually, with no real effort to define the role as unique. By making her my animal, I had a tabula rasa to define my expectations, and thus her expectations of herself. The word "slave" had baggage, and had been drained of meaning by common usage, so I discarded it.

The Forked Tongue

"Animal" was suggestive of the position that she would hold in my life, and from the very instant I first used it, helped shape her expectations:

Do animals get a vote?

Do animals eat at the same table?

Do they automatically get a bed, or sleep with their owner?

Are they *peers*?

These things were established effortlessly from the beginning, because her sense of self *in relation to me* was not set as that of an equal. It was that of my Animal. Her self-esteem and sense of self to the rest of the world was untouched if not enhanced; there was only one person she was ever obliged to take shit from, and she was his animal. The rest of the world had best step aside. (I like when what is on my leash has sharp teeth – and she does, in spades. It's a useful trait and an admirable quality no matter what side of the leash you are on. I'd rather have an attack dog than a poodle any day.)

I addressed her only as "animal". To call her by her given name would have been (and once was) a crushing, savage blow. I reinforced the idea of what was expected of a good animal at every opportunity, creating an axis of success and failure based on the identity, reshaping her in many ways to meet my expectations. It was not a complete brainwash by any means; there were many core values I could never change – but I could often fit those values into the Animal/Owner relationship, absorbing what I could not alter. She is Animal to me to this day, and no matter how our relationship continues to evolve, I suspect that will never change.

Overcoming Previous Conditioning

Regardless of whether it is previous relationships, intentional conditioning, or just life as it's been lived, anyone you deal with will come with some conditioning which are not to your best interest. Again, I have no sure-fire cure-all, but I can suggest a technique that has produced good results for me in the past.

NEVER ATTACK A PRECONDITIONED RESPONSE HEAD ON.

One of the factors of long-standing conditioning is that if it is deep enough or lasts long enough, it becomes incorporated into your subject's self-image. It becomes *how they think of themselves*. This is to your advantage as you reinforce your own conditioning, but may be in your way when it is a pre-existing condition. The principle to keep in mind is one of misdirection. Addressing the condition head-on is akin to saying "*Don't think about the elephant.*" The subconscious does not process negatives that way, all you'll be doing is reinforcing the condition by harping on it, and creating stress and angst as, in all likelihood, it gets worse and more sensitive and troublesome. What you are seeking to do is *replace* the condition, by reinforcing a different context entirely.

Now, this cannot always be done, but your chances are better the more deeply layered your efforts and misdirection are. If, for example, boot kissing has powerful negative associations for your servant because of previous negative experience, you might try to address it like this:

> Address concern about the condition of your boots – make certain that they are placed in a specific place every night, for example. Give the servant errands to run which concern your boot, such as – picking up boot care products, taking them for repair and upkeep, replacing used brushes and the like.

> Instruct your servant in leather care and bootblacking. If your servant has a possessive streak, you might exploit it by considering aloud having others attend to the boots, and express approval of the job that others do, especially in a D/s context.

Seat your servant at your feet in moments of intimacy, instructing him to bring you the boots when it is time to put them on and remove them at the end of the day in a ritualized fashion.

When disappointed or displeased, do not allow the servant to perform these services. Reframe contact with your boots as a *privilege*.

All of these things, over time, will indelibly associate you, your authority, and your pleasure and approval (as well as your disapproval when appropriate) with the boots. The boots and the accompanying rituals will come to symbolize you, to be equated with you. When I have been away, I have given a servant a boot to keep, attend to, and even *sleep with* in my absence. I want that association to be *indelible*. One could also use the principles of redefinition, making the boots a central part of the servant's sense of self and function in relation to you. As this cements, it is very likely to erode the previous conditioning, until the boot-kissing may even be volunteered as a tribute – the boots are indelibly associated with you, they *are* you.

Perhaps you could get the servant to kiss the boot by simply demanding it, and spare yourself all the trouble, but that will not inspire *enthusiasm*; it will not inspire the *desire* to do it.

Now we have some language and some free floating ideas – what do we *do* with them? It's pretty obvious that this kind of thing requires a strategy, a plan to tackle such a big issue. Luckily, the world is filled with models and patterns for just this kind of thing. The real convenience of these frameworks is not that the work is done for you – it's not – but that these are *archetypes*, archetypes that come with their own weight, language and expectations. By using these models to start with you can often bridge otherwise vast gulfs of understanding and connection between you and your subject, because they come with preset senses of *what is expected*. They can be a common reference point to build from.

The Military Model is an excellent example. After WWII, the gay leather vets formed their secretive circles around this model more often than not – a common experience built around rank, hierarchy, trial, masculinity, and obedience. It was custom built for kink, and was a common language among everyone involved. It can still serve that function now, as even those who have never served in the military have some idea of the structure and expectations, the essential *values*. In training my boi, I used the military model as a common point of reference, along with the kink culture of the leathermen and cycle clubs (which themselves descended from the military model to a greater or lesser degree).

The Animal Model is also pretty universal, but contains a lot more room for personal interpretation and thus, possible miscommunication. Be clear if you are thinking "beast of burden," that your servant is not thinking "pampered pet" or "lap cat." But that aside, the fundamental imagery and expectations – and thus the *definition* – is easy to share. For example, if you designate that someone is your "pig," you have a fine starting point of shared concepts to build your vision from.

Caste/Historical Models abound, they just take a bit of homework. Odds are good if an era or culture fascinates you, you've already done much of the research. A good example is the **Dojo Model**, where the elements of the traditional martial arts power imbalance between Sensei and student are clear, well defined, and already demand respect, obedience, formality, tradition, and physical and mental trial – and *striving for approval.* Pre-revolutionary France, American slavery, Indian caste systems... the human race has been subjugating one or another element of itself on each other as a way of life since the beginning, and much of it is well documented. If history and culture can be used to reset a servant's expectations of themselves in relation to you, then it is of potential use.

Fetish models are the most widely referenced, yet shallowest pool to take from. An entire sub-subculture of "Gorean" D/s has evolved, modeled in varying degrees on the John Norman science fiction Gor novels – a common language with understandable expectations is very appealing, even to many who do not even recognize the potential power they hold with the shared fantasy. **The Story of O** is another fine example of fiction that sets parameters and expectations, a crowbar into the mind and identity of those who have shared the experience, if you but decide to make the effort to exert the leverage.

Family Models are powerful in every life, and in many ways evolve to some degree in every relationship. The question here is if you choose to exploit that power – although be aware, it may come saddled with unique and equally powerful baggage. Curiously, family models are often made just as powerful by their historical absence as they are by a positive history or even a negative one. Take the classic "Daddy" role – power without need for justification and authority are essential parts of the context. Where a benevolent, loving father may have left a positive association and desire to please, a negative one may have left scarring that aches for the catharsis of redefinition, and an absent one left a needy void to be filled. More than any other, the family model is *universal.*

IMPRINTING (THE MAGIC BULLET)

We can't discuss conditioning without touching on *imprinting*. Imprinting is an unpredictable factor in human nature. It happens under intense negative stress with some consistency, but it is nothing you can force, nothing you can count on. Imprinting is deep conditioning that just *happens*. In addition, it manifests in unpredictable ways. Someone who narrowly escapes death by drowning may have no lasting fear of water, but may be horrified by the sound of a buoy or the *smell* of seawater. I bring it up because it can happen even in utterly unexpected circumstances. At one point, I whispered something into my animal's ear at a movie theatre. Like magic it *imprinted*, and became an indelible part of our relationship structure. *Pow*.

My only advice about imprinting is this: the more you condition a subject, the more susceptible to your conditioning they become. Therefore – be careful of what you do and in what context you do it, as the deeper you go into a servant's mind, the more likely you are to leave lasting bootprints.

Knowing that lets me sleep at night. *Smiling.*

A NOTE ABOUT STANDARDS

Keep them hoping, keep them striving. If they become perfect in something, raise the bar or work on whatever comes next. No one is ever *done*, they are with you to be *given* hoops to jump through. If you suddenly say *"That's it – no more hoops."* complacency will set in, which leads to erosion and eventually disintegration. When you are single, diet and appearance have a specific importance – but what tends to happen once people marry and settle down? It's human nature, and it is up to you to spearhead the fight against it. Sadly, being a good Dominant is not just leaning back and being fed grapes and fanned with big feathers. Work, work, work.

The Forked Tongue

Chapter 6: Interrogation
As Old As Secrets

Why Interrogation?

Up until this point, nothing in **The Forked Tongue** has had a script, a step-by- step "Here's what you do." It has all been a matter of my outlining tools, and your deciding what it suits you to do with them. Despite appearances, this chapter is at heart no different. I will be outlining terms and tools, but in this case I will be assembling them in a specific order. The reason for this is to watch many of the tools that we have discussed in previous chapters used together, in a proven science, as a functional whole.

Do your research: Do I know what I am getting into?

If you are going to undertake this sequence, it is vital that you know your source. This is not a scene to be undertaken casually. All the ideas I addressed on this under Mindfucks are even more important here, as where Mindfucking can be scary, it is playful in comparison with Interrogation. This is the science of ruin; and with the wrong source – a source who cannot look back on the experience and be moved and grateful for every terrible minute of the experience – you are facing disaster, and terrible consequences for everyone involved.

Keep your own limitations in mind. There is a lot riding on this, and if you have a feeling that your credibility as a Dominant is riding on the enterprise, then you are not far from wrong. So as you consider, plan and prepare, be certain you can go through with what you undertake, and be sure you do not overstep yourself – your abilities, your comfort zone, or the sacred framework of your structure for fear of failure. Know what you can do, and be confident you can handle a person who is not in his normal state of mind – and that you are more than capable of picking up the pieces afterward.

Finally, do not be confused by the *appearances* of your effort – don't be distracted by the very actions you undertake. This is about the *state of mind you create in your source.* Nothing else.

KNOW YOUR SOURCE.

KNOW YOURSELF.

KNOW YOUR GOALS.

I've been asked: if this is such potentially dangerous stuff, why tell people about it? *Because all the information is already out there.* Where do you think I got it? So, what I have done is rendered the information into tools and a sequence which the top can control to *prevent* disaster – because simply following the easily accessible cookbook recipe for interrogation/deprogramming can only lead to ruin and worse.

Okay. I'm done with the warnings. Sit up, pay attention – let's do this.

Locked doors, bright lights, rubber hoses... props are easy, but that's not what makes an interrogation. It is a science as old as secrets, with useful, applicable tools and principles, which are useful anywhere from bedrooms to cellars to closets to club corners.

For as long as there have been tribes, there has been territory, and as long as there has been territory, there has been the fight to keep it... and the key to that fight, and all such fights, is *information.* Humans were trying to pry secrets from each other while they were still using bones and flint tools. The science of interrogation was well underway when all science was looked at as the work of the Devil; and scientific advances have never failed to find their way into the interrogator's hands.

This book is written for Tops, but it's sure to find its way into the hands of bottoms who can't resist the lure of the topic, relishing the terrible masochistic details of the topic; fantasy fodder of the purest sort.

That's not a problem.

The science *works*. It works if you know; it works if you don't. The only differences are time and application. Soldiers are prepared with all the information you'll get here and far, far more... but in the end: *everybody talks*. It's science, it's gravity. It's inevitable. All you need is time, privacy, patience, and a few tools... the tools I am providing here.

Definitions:

Debility *n: The state of being weak; weakness; feebleness; languor.*

The idea of *debility* is more far-reaching in interrogation than in most bondage/scene activities. Where restraint can run the length of a scene – or *be* the scene – debility is more far-reaching, more akin to *captivity*. The entire environment of your subject (or *source*) becomes your leverage. It is this factor that makes an interrogation scenario unique: the total immersion of your subject is your goal, for hours or days at a time.

Dependency *n: 1. Lack of independence or self-sufficiency; 2. Being abnormally dependent on something that is psychologically or physically habit-forming.*

To regress your subject to conditions of infancy, dependent on you for food, water, being clean, being warm, being allowed to sleep, utterly subject to the whims of the superior. This environment inevitably creates an eagerness to please, as that is the only chance the subject has to find comfort, ease, or dignity. This is best achieved through *Debility*, above.

The Forked Tongue

Dread *v:* *To fear in a great degree; to regard, or look forward to, with terrific apprehension.*

What you *might* do is always more frightening than what you have done. Especially in a situation where certain means (such as execution, or permanent captivity) are not as applicable as they would be for, say, our armed forces. Suspense is a torture unto itself, a weight which will eventually buckle even the strongest knees. Your goal is to create that suspense, that *dread*. Dread is different than terror – terror can galvanize a weakening will. The adrenaline and power of instinct can work against you. Dread is weakening, debilitating. The hollowness of the stomach, the weakening of the knees and will... these are the effects of dread applied correctly.

Doubt *v:* *To waver in opinion or judgment; to be in uncertainty as to belief respecting anything; to hesitate in belief; to be undecided as to the truth of the negative or the affirmative proposition; to be undetermined.*

In a situation which, in the end, is consensual, you will be acting against the knowledge that your subject does, in fact, trust – and possibly love – his/her Interrogator. This person may have a very good idea of you, of what your limits are, may have faith that you would never really do anything too terrible, that this is just a fun ride to take together – and in the end, so it is. But to make it so, there must be a *suspension of disbelief*, a *doubt* of the things that your subject knows to be true. Not a shattering of faith, *never* a betrayal – but *doubt*. There must be nothing safe but that which you designate as safe.

Source: From the KUBARK manuals of the CIA (recently declassified) comes the term "source." It is here going to be used as the blanket term for slave/submissive/boy/boi/girl/subject/captive/servant/whatever. The term is gender neutral, and to the point: Boys, girls and submissives are *people*. Sources are a *resource*. And although you may know and love this person, once you give the impression that you see them only as a *resource*... the fun has already started. So we'll use the term *"source"* from here on in.

The Relevancy of Information

Don't be distracted by the facts.

For our purposes, this is *not* actually about extracting information. That is the illusion that you are maintaining in order to craft an *experience* for your source. I very strongly recommend that you do not apply these techniques to extract information which is actually being withheld from you, that will compromise your judgment, and that is something you **cannot** afford. The fact is, information is not relevant to the actual process at hand, and actively pursuing something which is being withheld from you commits you to a pass/fail situation which you do not want to be in. If you wish to break it down further, the actual pursuit of information puts your source in charge. *They* have something *you* want. That's leverage, and an invitation to bad judgment all the way around. If you use the methods I suggest, you run no risk of failure, as you are *not actually seeking information*. **Information is an illusion**. I don't know about you, but I hate to lose – so I stack the deck before the game even starts.

Creating the Sequence

Arrest

The first step of the sequence is arrest. By this I mean a *shocking disruption of routine*. If the intent is to disorient the source, interrupting their sleep – especially around 3am, when the body is at its lowest ebb – is a tried and true method. This is not a sequence you start after a nice dinner, a glass of wine and some mood music. The introduction should be jarring and unfamiliar. I have also found that (especially when kicking in someone's door at 3am is legally inadvisable) mealtimes are a good choice. People tend to let their guard down, as these are traditionally relaxing times, *safe* times.

So; prepare the nice dinner, pour some wine, light some candles – and in the *middle* of the entrée, drop a bag over his head and zip tie his hands behind his back. Don't worry about the leftovers, they'll keep. Blow out the candles and it's time to move on to the next step.

DETENTION

The next step is to hold your source in an unfamiliar environment. *Detention* is an important stage, as it is a passive reinforcement for the source that the situation – that her *life* – is no longer under her own control in any way.

Now, we don't all have access to an abandoned warehouse, isolated storage container, or hidden basement cell, so we have to make do with what we can. If you can't procure a strange space, make a familiar space strange. Quietly clean out a basement space or a closet in *advance*. Move all the furniture out of the guest room. If you have sufficient privacy, drag her outside, toss her in the back seat and cover her with something, drive around awhile and then bring her in – still hooded – through a *different exit* than you left. If you have homey touches like wind chimes or a screen door, get them out of the way before you move your source. Even hooded, they will be straining their senses for the familiar – scents, a sequence of steps, the sounds of a neighbor's pet – *any* straw she can grasp to tell her where she is. Do your prep work, don't give her that straw. Even better, have a friend prepare a closet or basement at their place. The more unfamiliar, the better.

The longer you can drag this segment out, the more effective it will be. Thirst, muscle aches, discomfort, and disorientation are your allies in this effort. Give no input, answer no questions, provide no comfort. This is time for **dread** to set in... let them enjoy it a while.

This time period is a special opportunity to *take things away*. This becomes important later on. Strip your source of all clothing and jewelry. If she wears makeup, scrub it off. Give him a t-shirt with a number to wear, and address him only by the number. Take away all the things that your source can measure *himself* by, if you can. There is a reason that prisons shave heads at intake, and it's not just head lice. Take these identifying, familiar tokens of *sense of self* away – you'll need them later.

THREATS, FEAR, AND YOU

Before we move forward with the sequence, we have to address a few factors in advance. I have mentioned this before, but it is worth mentioning again: **There is nothing more disempowering than an empty threat**. If you keep your threats vague, or unspoken, you can get a lot of mileage out of the building dread. You don't have to say anything if you bring in a car battery, jumper cables, and a bucket of water, and leave them out of reach, but in sight. Illusion and props.

If you commit to a verbal threat, you will lose ground if your source does not believe you can or will carry it through. So be careful what you say.

Menacing your source with a truly terrible object can cause fear and panic – and panic escalates a situation right out of your control. So, if you want to scare your source with a pair of hedge clippers, don't brandish them – just leave them in sight and say nothing about them. In the middle ages, torturers would lay the tools of their trade out to be seen by their victims, to allow the dread to build. Dread is better than fear, as I've mentioned before. Fear spikes, burns out, and may even build resolve. Dread weakens, debilitates, and *erodes* resolve. So in everything you do until the very end, always leave yourself some room to escalate. Calm is better than shouting; slow and deliberate is better than sudden. Take your time, time is your friend.

The Forked Tongue

Pain is a tempting tool – but don't use it right away, don't overuse it, and don't stake everything on it. Pain can be endured, defeated – and that can improve resolve. The threat and fear of pain is more effective for our purposes than pain itself. If and when you do decide to inflict pain, again, don't get confused by your own performance – this is not about actually obtaining information. This is about *state of mind*.

QUESTIONING

What makes an interrogation scene different from simple abduction and abuse is *questioning*. It is the stagecraft of an interrogation, and it takes some skill, preparation, and invention. A healthy dose of improvisation is helpful as well, but what I am going to lay out here are the tools for you to make a powerful and lasting impact through your inquiries.

First choose the *relevant fact.* Note, this is *not "what you want to know,"* since there is actually *nothing* that you want to know – you already have your answers. But there needs to be a central fact for you to work around.

For example, let's say you know your source went out last Friday night. You've done a little homework, and know who she went with and what they did, and that they ran into a third party you both know. Harmless.

You choose a fact from these: the third party, a minor incidental detail.

That is the one thing you do not ask about.

Instead, prepare about five questions which revolve *around* that fact:

Where did you go?

Who did you go with?

Have you ever been there before?

What did you do with them?

When was that?

You can complicate and deepen the questioning process in many ways, all really good devices to keep you from sounding like a broken record, repeating yourself over and over until you sound silly even to yourself. You can employ multiple lines of questioning, for example; instead of only one set of associated questions, how about three *unrelated* sets? Don't be afraid to write and keep notes, and use them as you grill your source; it only adds to the illusion, rather than detract from it. Ask a question a few times, and then let on that you knew the answer already, and in greater detail than your source had given you. It promotes a menacing sense of omniscience.

As you ask these questions, follow the leads for facts that they offer. Keep careful note of those facts. If you have an opportunity to ask about several similar events, so much the better. Ask about them in a non-linear fashion, blaming any confusion you deliberately inspire on an unwillingness to tell the truth. Go over details again and again, making efforts to confuse, muddle, and if you need to, willfully misinterpret the answers you get, circling around and around your central fact, but *never asking it*. You are the authority figure in a Kafka nightmare. If you are skilled at such things, you can devise a series of inquiries which lead to incorrect conclusions or misstatements, or use syllogisms. (A syllogism is a word trap such as *"All cats die, Socrates is dead, so now you are saying Socrates was a cat?"*) If you break these leading questions up among other questions, the source will never see it coming.

This is often the time to employ "**The Forked Tongue,**" the infuriating argument tactic the book is named for. You have set up your four or five lines of questioning, and your source is desperately attempting to give an answer which will please you, mollify you, make you ease up on her. When she answers one question, hit her with another, in an accusatory fashion.

"What does that have to do with where you went?"

"That does not answer the question of who you went with."

"That answer does not address the question of your having been there before."

"Why are you not telling me what did you did with them?"

"What I wanted to know is when this occurred. You are not being straight with me"

This way, any time the source gives you her best answer to a question, no matter how truthful – it is still *never enough*. It's like slapping someone's hand when they reach out to take something you have offered. It can help you reinforce the feelings of despair, dread, and futility, and can keep you from getting bogged down in the facts, such as the fact that this person is telling you the truth. The truth does not matter, the state of mind you invoke is the only thing that matters.

Occasionally reward random facts or answers with minor comforts – sips of water, a trip to the bathroom. Respond to other answers – or the same answers, at another time – with negative reinforcements of slowly escalating unpleasantness and severity. This is *meant* to be unfair, to be hopeless. Offer just enough occasional rewards that there is a glimmer of hope that there *is* a right answer, if only your source can give it to you. You are pushing your source to despair, to the point where he will say anything, confess to anything, just for a reprieve, an answer, to be *safe*.

What do you do when you get there, to that state where you are satisfied that your source is where you want him?

Go over your facts one more time, this time in a linear order. (This will start the process of restoring order to your source's universe, but this is only the beginning.) This is when you ask about that *central fact* – the one question you have *never asked*. This is how you control the pacing, how it is that you control when the scene begins and ends – **by not asking the question of what you really *"wish to know"* until you are ready.**

After you have gotten your answer, give something back. Return bits of comfort and identity, one step at a time, as you ask about the details of the central fact. (In the case of our example, the chance meeting with the third party.) Address this as a debriefing, but it really is a return to reality, safety, and equilibrium. As the answers come, return things – things like items of clothing, jewelry, eventually leading up to your source's name – the last and most intimate thing you can return. This slow return to equilibrium is an important process – you cannot just yank the curtain back and say *"It's over – let's go get pizza."* I have had a source who did not believe it was over just because I said so – you have dismantled this person's world, and he will need your help in returning it to order. It is also a profound bonding experience, and a remarkable opportunity to reinforce positive redefinition as your slave, boy, pet, or what have you. (We addressed this sort of redefinition in Chapter 5: Conditioning.) You have broken him down – it's an ideal time to rebuild him that much more to your liking.

You see why I say this is not a casual scene? Done correctly, it will have ramifications which carry through and help define your relationship for a long time to come. It will also have long-lasting effects if executed poorly, but those are not likely the results you are seeking.

Variants

There are many different ways to approach your interrogation, different methods that suit your personal style, the vulnerabilities and fantasies of your source, or that you just think might be amusing. Some of the possibilities include:

- **Multiple Interrogators**

    Good Cop/Bad Cop is a classic – and it's a classic because it works. It becomes especially effective if you have a Dominant friend who your source is afraid of, or conversely is *less* afraid of than you, and thus might make an appropriate Good Cop. Personally, I *love* playing Good Cop. I think it's that look of hope that dawns on the face of the source when she thinks she might be getting out – and the look that replaces it when I regretfully inform her that her claims don't add up with the information I have, and that if she's going to be that uncooperative, she's going to have to deal with my associate.

    The fact is there are no "Good Cops;" but slowly the feeling grows that no matter how bad you are, you are the best hope they have...

- **Alice In Wonderland**

    Alice is the method of combining the reality alteration of a mindfuck with the breaking down of an interrogation. By asking questions and making accusations that have no grounding in reality, especially if you start slowly and gradually replace the reasonable, answerable questions with "facts" and conclusions based on those facts that have nothing to do with anything that has actually occurred, you may be able to make the source doubt herself, her memory and her sanity. In the end, someone with nothing real to hold on to will confess to anything. Props and other staged "proof" – including the testimony of others – are especially effective.

    Sometimes the battery of unanswerable questions alone can create the cathartic "release" of confession in your source. Captured Air Force pilots who were interrogated behind the Iron Curtain during the Cold War reported being forced to stand at rigid attention for hours on end (euphemistically called "stress positions" nowadays) while enduring a fierce, aggressive barrage of questions they *could not possibly answer*. Hour after hour of exhausting abuse, the interrogators would ask questions that the captive *could* answer. Often the relief of being able to say something, *anything* to alleviate the situation overwhelmed other judgment, and the exhausted pilots would answer anything they could - gratefully.

Summation

There are many different places to get ideas and practical information, ranging from hard reference texts and handbooks (check online book retailers, there are *dozens*) to popular media. Television and movies may be more helpful than you might imagine - the various *Law and Order* shows and *The Closer* base much of their interrogation sequences on actual police tactics. *The Spanish Prisoner* and *Closetland* are entire films dedicated to interrogations, and the scene where Agent Smith questions Neo in *The Matrix* is an excellent demonstration of an interrogator appearing in control, having "all the facts," and remaining calm and measured while being menacing.

Regardless of the methods you choose and the props and illusions you construct, the key to a successful interrogation is always the same: know your source, know yourself, and *control the pacing to control the outcome*. Never ask *"the real question"* until you are ready to get an answer, and be prepared to help rebuild whatever you tear down.

In Conclusion

I have gone this whole book without moralizing or getting on a soapbox about safety, and I intend to stay that way. But I will allow myself this: in an interrogation, if you are uncertain, *err on the side of caution*. The experience you create will be memorable - but what kind of memorable relies entirely on your good judgment. There are no safewords here; you are both working the high wire without a net. But the experiences that you can craft with the right person and some diligent, passionate work are legendary – and quite literally world-changing for all involved.

Maybe you don't want to go that far. It's not safe, and it is not universally rewarding. In fact the sort of people on either side of the leash who really *want* or *need* to walk these paths are few and far between. But here you are, with *The Forked Tongue* in your hands. You have read this far, and it is for *one reason*, no matter what you tell yourself. If you are slowing down to stare at a car wreck, you might tell yourself it's out of concern, or fear, or habit – but in the end, any fascination means *you are interested*.

You *want* to know.

It will go easier for you if you just admit it.

Chapter 7: The Last Word
Edgeplay, Life and Death

The word "edgeplay" does not really have – like most terms in use in this community – a consistent definition. Some people consider things "edgy" that others do twice before breakfast. Subjective and charged, the word carries connotations which can only complicate actual exploration. So I want to posit a definition for use, if only here and now:

Edgeplay is playing with *risk* – with the threat or certainty of losing something meaningful or permanent.

This idea covers the common thread which loosely links the activities which are most often addressed as "edge." In every case, there is *something to lose*. Social position, liberty, physical health, mental health, or life itself; they are all fair game when it comes to playing the edge. This book has been an exploration of mental edgeplay; in every case each player risks loss or even ruin. On the surface. It might appear that only the bottom is in danger – but edgeplay can have consequences, *profound* consequences – on either side of the leash.

In previous chapters we have addressed mental edgeplay concepts such as humiliation, interrogation, mindfucks, conditioning and the like – and there are others. Abuse play, incest games, and other forms of dark, emotionally charged role playing, the devastating impact of emotional sadomasochism; the variations are as endless as the individuals involved.

There are environmental edges to ride, such as captivity. Permanent physical modifications, ranging from piercing and tattoos to castration. Physical risk: gunplay, knifeplay, breathplay, fireplay, some suspension and advanced ropework; even structural edgeplay: consensual *non-consent*. All of these things carry risk, the potential of loss and ruin, each in it's own individual way. Rather than attempt to explore or even explain every variation, it is the *concept* I wish to address, and the questions that concept inevitably raises:

- *In any relationship, people change each other. Is it wrong to do it intentionally?*
- *What about your social responsibilities to your gender/race/ orientation/faith?*
- *What gives you the right to do this to someone else?*
- *Does a person have the right to take these risks or allow these changes within his/herself?*
- *Does a person have the right to take these risks or cause these changes within another?*
- *Where does the law come in to these decisions?*
- *How much of a consideration is the State?*

Honestly, I don't think these questions matter. The debates are as subjective as the topic. People intentionally set out to change each other all the time, here we are at least ethically addressing that possibility (or certainty) up front, within the initial creation of structure. Responsibilities to gender, faith, or race? These are either personal, private choices to be made by the individual, or they are bludgeons being used by those with an agenda. Either way, the point is again unfit for general debate.

What gives me the *right*?

Who I am in relation to my servants. I *don't* have the right to do this to just anybody (not that I would, I try to keep myself a more valuable commodity than that). I am not attacking strangers – I am imposing my will on those who have come to me – and stay with me – for that specific purpose. So the question becomes "Do they have the right to have this done to them? Do they have the right to seek their own sacrament, to seek what makes them whole?"

Damn right they do. If you don't like it, don't do it – but that's as far as anybody else's opinion reaches in these matters.

What about the law? What about the state?

What about them?

As the bottom takes chances in these matters, so does the top. There are things described in this book and mentioned in this chapter that risk life, limb, and liberty for those involved. And you know what?

That's the *point*.

Do you drive? Take the subway? Go to concerts or clubs? Eat food other people have prepared?

How many times a day is your life in the hands of people you will never know, never meet? Fire inspectors, chefs, customs agents, elevator technicians, medical professionals – and those are the ones that may be in some way *accountable*. Armed strangers, poor drivers, drunken idiots – our lives are constantly intersecting with others who have the power to do us harm. We don't think about it, or we'd never get through the day – but we are all one drug addled subway driver, one overworked air traffic controller, one careless speeder away from disaster.

The Forked Tongue

How do you take back what the world takes from you? How do you reclaim what the world takes from you every day – control over your own fate?

You *choose*. You choose to entrust your fate to a specific person, someone you have designated. You walk the tightrope on *your own terms* for once. The skydiver, the race driver, the free climber have all known this: You celebrate being alive by risking it all.

All the questions about edgeplay come down to one frightened cry: *"How can you do this?"*

The only reply that matters is *"How can I **not**?"*

Be true to who you are. Act ethically, choose carefully, and be true.

Flagg
New York City, 2008

Afterward:
Unalterable, Unforgettable, Unforgivable

"He who makes a beast of himself gets rid of the pain of being a man."
-Dr. Johnson

Hunter S. Thompson opened his book **Fear and Loathing in Las Vegas** with this quote; I suspect that Dr. Thompson knew a great deal more about his Beast than most people are likely to fathom. He described himself as "violent" and "explosive" in his letters, well aware of a feral, raging, aggressive element of himself that he exorcised in person and on paper, striking out at the elements of a society he saw as corrupt, stupid, or even worse – complacent. Dealing with Dr. Thompson in person was likened to making friends with a minefield; if you survived the initial contact you were good to go, provided you watched where you stepped.

About a decade ago I joined TES (A historic BDSM support organization based in NYC), seeking wisdom and experience. I thought that I would find elders there, "Tom-of-Finland" style leathermen who knew all the secrets, all the answers. I was, of course, wrong. How could any stranger answer the questions which consumed me? The questions were not about BDSM, or culture, or kink – they were about me, what I wanted, what I hungered for, and what I was unable to face about myself. In my third year, I had put in enough time to know the smell of what I wanted, to start stirring those dark waters, however cautiously. I had done a presentation on knife and fear play; one of the statesmen of the group, a 30-year fixture of the place, stopped me:

> *"How do you actually do it?"* he asked in the hall after the presentation. *"I mean, you know her, she knows you; she knows you are not going to kill her, so why should she be afraid?"*

> *"You have to mean it."* I said.

> No answer at all and the only one that counts.

It was at that moment, as I looked into his uncomprehending eyes and saw no possible way of explaining anything about it to him, that I realized my feelings of isolation and difference were not elitism, not arrogance, not insecurity but something else, something *genuine*. This man would never understand. Very few people would. We were all here, we went to the same parties, wore the same clothes, attended the same meetings... but we were *not the same*. Some of us were as different as divergent species, like dogs and wolves. It was at that point I set about seeking my own kind; and as rare as they were, they were recognizable a mile off. I could *smell* them. Like some kind of biblical Mark of Caine, they'd *shine*. So I started to assemble family, pack – and started talking to people who seemed to be a dark reflection of the things that drove me, a kinship which transcended more common differences. Unlikely associations developed, because none of the labels or barriers mattered in comparison to this feeling of *recognition*.

But pack were, and are, few and far between.

Not everyone clicks. Not everyone so marked becomes pack or family, we are still people after all – but that sense of identification is there, concrete, and tends to carry its own regard. We may not even *like* each other, but we know in the end that we are some kind of kin. "You can't pick your family" runs true, even here. Defining what exactly it is that links us is a little more abstract, a little harder to define.

I've said that for me, BDSM is about making my demons pull the wagon, instead of chasing me – or worse, dragging me along behind them. Making these things that make me *different*, maybe *bad*, a positive part of who I am and what I do. Making these things, somehow, work *for* me after all this time. What it took to get here, to reverse this burden was **acceptance**. That was much harder than it sounds. Not the acceptance of "the community" – I sought that first, and receiving it left me hollow and troubled. I could play the reindeer games, but they meant nothing to me; they were a mockery of whatever it was that was restlessly moving around inside me. Acceptance by those few found peers was and is integral to the process, but that in itself was not near enough, it just meant that I was not alone in being alone. During this time I was lucky enough to find two close peers to talk to, and that's where the real work began: **acceptance of my own desires**.

When I came out into the public scene, I began with a quickly accelerating scale of physical sadism. I was blessed with a partner who was unaware of the depths of her own masochism, and who had a perversely playful sensibility. We quickly abandoned the prevailing standards of our community and gained the benefits of local notoriety. Physical sadism, it seemed, was acceptable, cool, even admired – provided it stayed within certain frameworks. It was those unspoken frameworks that began to chafe:

> *Scenes start and stop visibly and clearly, and to press the idea of authority outside those times is bordering on abuse. Real authority does not exist, it is an illusion created to allow for kink. To pursue it is to be overbearing, to be "taking it all too seriously."*

> *Kink is a game. Kink should not touch the sanctity of day-to-day life, and it always comes second. Anything further is pretentious and unrealistic. In the end, it's role-play.*

> *The bottom's feelings are paramount in any conflict; any other interpretation is abuse. In the end, she is doing me a favor; I should keep that in mind lest she stop.*

The Forked Tongue

> *In the end, nobody really wants to hurt anybody.*

Not enough. Nowhere *near* enough. Just enough to let me know what I was not getting, to make the sense of emptiness become clear. But it was with this partner that I had my first epiphany, my first real clue. Because though I knew things were missing, I was not ready to admit what was missing to myself. These things would make me a *bad person*, it was not *right* to want them.

I stood in Hellfire (a NYC BDSM club), my girl Tink perched on a padded bench, gone wherever it is masochists go. I looked at my hands, my shirt, my boots... they were spattered with blood. A pool of blood was forming on the floor where I stood. In realistic terms, it was nothing, but at that moment, it looked like a hemorrhage. Deep inside me, something *shifted*, and spoke.

It said "*Yes.*"

Describing it later, I called it my "Inner Serial Killer," and I was only half-joking. It was a blissful awareness that something was not *right* inside me... but for the first time, that something could be *fed* without my losing myself to it. It was the first moment of truce between me and the things that prowled in the back of my head making me uncomfortable, afraid of myself. It was the first element I recognized, consciously, of what I wanted out of the circus of floggers and parlor tricks that surrounded me. I wanted what I did to *matter*. I wanted what I did to be *real*, like the blood was real.

But if not blood for blood's sake, then what?

About that time, I was fortunate enough to recognize kin for the first time. Soulhuntre and I butted heads until mutual respect and a shared sense of humor and perversity won out – but from the first, we recognized something akin within each other. It was he who offered me a singularly valuable perspective:

> *I did not have to play by their rules.*

It's amazing to me in retrospect what a *shock* this was. I had sought and romanticized this community for so long, I had simply accepted its taboos and customs as law, without thought, without debate. I so wanted to belong to something, this fantasy Holy Land of like-minded souls, that I was ignoring the fact that on the whole, they were *not* like-minded. As I did not know my own mind, I accepted theirs. I was sacrificing something about myself for *acceptance*. Not only that, I could blame those taboos for my not exploring the parts of myself that drove me, kept me awake, made me unhappy, unfed, unfulfilled, unspeakable. *They* would not let me, so I did not have to.

Suddenly, I did not have that excuse. Not only that, I had a peer – a person to whom it seemed I might be able to talk about the unspeakable, almost to *confess* to without fearing judgment – for it seemed that his demons drove him as hard as mine drove me. He was in no position to judge me, and that made it safe. Soon we were joined by one more, Sir C, and together, the three of us tried to change our world to suit our own image. What really happened, though, is that we grew up together, getting to know ourselves through each other. There is no way to encapsulate the variety of experience and growth of that time. Instead, I'll focus on the lessons:

Their rules don't matter. My rules, and the integrity of those rules, do.

What I want is not to role play. Ever. It is to rule, with genuine effect and authority in the lives of the people under me, in exactly the way I had been told was entirely wrong.

There are people out there who want what I have, what I am. Those people are worth waiting for. That those who do not understand are not worth expending energy on, for there is no return on the investment.

That pain is a tool. Not an end. Pain matters only when it has purpose, when it allows me deeper into the head, heart, and soul of the person under me. If that connection is not there, it was worse than useless; it was a waste of time.

The Forked Tongue

That I would never stop being greedy to get further and further inside. That no invasion was enough.

That I wanted to make changes. Profound, permanent changes. That my satisfaction came from leaving irrevocable boot prints in the minds of those under me. That I was not satisfied with shaping their behavior – that I wanted to shape and mark their nature. To break the cardinal rules on every level.

Unalterable, unforgettable, unforgivable.

Still, I was not done.

It was not pain or violence that inspired me, it was not control; these are things I understood, that I had befriended, striving to further myself, to pull my wagon. But there was something else, and it was what I wanted most, so it was what I buried deepest. Two defining relationships of my life – my *beggar child* and my *animal* -- were the vessels of these new lessons, of the next stage of growth. In each of them I was forced to face my desires – and the lies I told myself to keep myself safe from my fear. Fear of conflict. Fear of going too far. Most of all, fear of being found unacceptable by those I loved.

As long as it went unexamined my fear would stay, making me afraid and ashamed of whom I am, what I want. Even now I am tempted not to name my wants here, not out of shame, but for fear of belittling them. In the end, it is not a big deal to anyone but me. But to me, it is *colossal*.

I grew up in a house of women: two sisters and my mother. I was a 70's child, raised on Alan Alda and female empowerment. Some things were sacred, including all things female; the only male figure in my life was belittled and despised; so I too assumed that mantle of contempt. On some level, I felt that being male was bad, contemptible: sins of the fathers. This was not something that was done to me intentionally; it was the confusion of a child and the baggage we carry into adolescence. At adolescence, the rage it engendered started to find a voice, which I suppressed. It was profane; it went against every value with which I had been raised with. It was *foul*.

That voice whispered *what I wanted*. Payback, certainly for the real and imagined indignities of childhood. But really, the source does not matter, only the effect does. Pain was a tool. It came close to where I wanted to go, but was no real answer in the end. Control was closer, more honest – but I was afraid to use that control to get what I really *wanted*, what my Beast required:

Crushing degradation. Humiliation. Objectification – every taboo of my upbringing. There was always a step lower, and there always will be. My kink revolves around who I am and who you are – and what I can do to make you smaller, make you look further and further up just to see my boots. No one can ever go low enough. As far as I can tell, this hunger has no limit. And I'm sure there is more I have not yet come to terms with. I can now accept this, although I do not always rest easy with aspects of it; like my taste for pain, like my desire to rule. I am not a bad person – but I *am*. And as long as I can decide for myself who I am to be, I will be a good man for it; I *choose* to be. I am not defined by my desires – but I recognize them. The danger that still remains is engendered by confusion. My animal pointed it out to me:

> *"Your 'Inner Serial Killer' is not the problem. Your need to humiliate and debase is not the problem. That's just you. It's your fear and guilt about it that's the problem."*

Simple. As long as I can remember that, the world makes sense.

I am no longer worried that I am a "serial killer waiting to happen." I know myself well enough that this is no longer a boogeyman. But I also recognize that many of the things that drive me are the same things that drive those monsters, that there is a sad and terrible kinship with our broken cousins who are dragged behind their demons, as they never had the good fortune and care that allows some of us to ride the wagon and choose our roads.

The Forked Tongue

They are broken, I am merely bent. And I have been blessed all along the way, with peers, and teachers that some people are never lucky enough to find. And I am not alone. I know you are out there.

I can *smell* you.

Flagg, March 2008
No Apologies

"You can turn your back on a person, but you can't turn your back on a drug. Especially when that drug is waving a razor sharp hunting knife in your eye"
Hunter S. Thompson, **Fear and Loathing in Las Vegas**

"You have to mean it."
Flagg

A Handbook for Treating People Badly

The Forked Tongue

Acknowledgements

A lot of people contributed to this effort, and there is no way to scale their efforts and importance – without any of them, this book might never have occurred.

To begin, I'd like to thank my Swamp Witch, Pixie, Punk, Beggar Child and Animal – every moment with each of you was enlightening, and like all enlightenment, beyond price.

To my sister Gail – when you found me and accepted who I had become, this project began.

To those I grew up with – Sir C and Soulhuntre, his girls Kimiko and Tatsumi, to my brother Daddy David and his girl Lexi, and to the Pack that has supported me unfailingly through the health crises which have defined my last few years – thank you. I don't know where I'd be without you, but I suspect it would be no place good.

A special mention to those who attempted to sacrifice their health and organs to try to help me – I will never, ever forget. Thank you.

Redhead Sue undertook the maddening prospect of editing this manuscript, Tatsumi gave it shape, and my oldest friend Danz took my vision for the cover design and made it sing, lending unique expertise and flawless vision. Soulhuntre made sure that it saw the light of day. Scottish Sam and Mistress Ardenne gave me valuable insights and motivation when I needed it.

All of you pitched in and worked hard to help me, and to make this book happen, and thus:

Look what you've done – you should be ashamed of yourselves.

Thank you.

Flagg
Foolish House
June 2008

The Forked Tongue

Made in the USA
Lexington, KY
03 July 2011